ART IN THE MOMENT

ART IN THE MOMENT

LIFE AND TIMES OF ADGER COWANS

by Adger Cowans,
as told to Peter Lownds

Noah's Ark Publishing Service
Beverly Hills, California

Art in the Moment: Life and Times of Adger Cowans

ISBN 978-1-7321325-3-5

NOAH'S ARK PUBLISHING SERVICE
8549 Wilshire Blvd. Suite 1442
Beverly Hills, CA 90211
www.lavaldreams.com

Edited by Brady Rhoades
Front cover photo of Adger Cowans by Mark Lee Blackshear

CONTENTS

My mother's family, the Watsons.

CHAPTER ONE

FAMILY

I was born in Columbus, Ohio in September 1936. My mother's name was Beatrice Louise Watson and my father's name was Adger W. Cowans. The name Adger was used as a surname by a family of French rugmakers. There was an American minister named John Bailey Adger who allowed African-Americans to sit with white folks in his church. My father was from Starr, South Carolina and my mother was from Belpre, Ohio. They got together and they married in 1931. They met in church. When he married my mother all her family, the Watsons, lived in Columbus. My father was a remarkable man. His father, "Big Jim" Cowans, married twice. When his mother died, my father, the oldest child, quit AT&T college and came back home. My aunt Gladys spoke with me at his funeral:

"You have no idea what kind of man your father was. He raised thirteen kids by himself. Grandpa Jim had to work, so your father fed us, he wiped our butts, he bathed us. He did everything."

My father was very serious when it came to taking care of his family. When he came north, he worked in the steel mills and then joined his brother, my uncle James, as a porter on the railroad. In Columbus, for many years, he worked for a wealthy white doctor and his family. He was in charge of the daily upkeep of the doctor's home, cooked three meals a day, made sure that the offices, the bedrooms, the kitchen, the whole place was in order, planted and maintained the spacious yards and gardens, washed the doctor's car, did everything but drive him around.

For a while, both my parents lived and worked in the family's mansion. Whenever the doctor, his wife, or children needed something, they rang a bell. My mother complained that she and my father were always on call, had no privacy or time of their own. Living on the line between service and servitude was intolerable. So they started looking for a house of their own where they could raise a family. My father ended up buying one from his uncle Sherrard, who owned the dry cleaning establishment where my father's youngest brother, Uncle James, worked.

My father was twelve years older than my mother. She was seeing someone else when she met my father but, as soon as she met him, she knew he was the one. Belpre, Ohio, where my mother was born, is down near Virginia. George Washington billeted his troops in the area when he was fighting the British. They included Native Americans, French, Irish, freed blacks, trappers, hunters and frontiersmen like Daniel Boone. My mother had indigenous American, French and African blood.

I grew up during the Second World War when every family in America had a ration book because "the best food was sent to the front lines for our boys fighting the war." We also had "tin drives" in school where people brought scrap metal to be used as ammunition. I remember when my uncles went off to war. My aunt Elizabeth stood me up on a covered radiator in front of the window of the Columbus railroad station and I could look down and see the soldiers getting on the train. The white soldiers got on the front of the train with seats and the black soldiers got on the back of the train in boxcars without seats. I remember looking down at my brand new shoes and hearing my aunt say, "It's a shame how they treat the colored soldiers!"

When I was little, my uncle Brad and aunt Thelma still lived in Belpre and we visited them frequently. Uncle Brad showed me the lean-to where my great-great grandfather had lived. They kept their hunting dogs there. Later on, they moved to the Bronx, a borough of New York City. Brad called her "Bimmie" and Thelma called him "Shug." Brad was a porter at Penn Station. He was known among his fellow porters for the beautiful introductions he would give out-of-towners when they arrived in Manhattan. He was proud of his adopted city.

When Grandpa George got a job on the Baltimore & Ohio Railroad, he moved the whole family from Belpre to Columbus, to a house at 1515 Harvard Street. That's where my mother and her four siblings were raised.

My father bought our house at 259 Taylor Avenue, which was only about three blocks from my mother's parents, Grandma Minnie and Grandpa George. My Grandpa George Watson's first wife, Maude, died after my Aunt Elizabeth was born. Grandma Minnie's father was white and her mother was black. She was "bought" by a wealthy black family who kept her chained to the bed at night so she wouldn't escape. After Maude's death, Grandpa George married her to help raise his children and keep his house. Grandma Minnie was a tough customer. She would pay me a little money to cut the grass and wash the windows and sit on the porch watching me like a hawk. If I overlooked anything, she let me know right away.

During and after the war, a lot of people raised chickens in their backyards. Grandma Minnie had a small vegetable garden with a chicken coop and she and Grandpa George rented half of their garage to a car mechanic, Mr. Covington. When Grandma asked you to go to the chicken coop to gather the eggs, the minute you opened the door the big black rooster would fly straight at you, spurs first. Everyone, even Grandpa George, was afraid of "that crazy old rooster." One day, when Grandma went out to get the eggs, the rooster flew at her. He got the surprise of his life. Grandma Minnie grabbed his neck in mid-air, wrung him around a few times and threw him down hard. Old Blacky's eyes wouldn't focus and he staggered around like a drunk. After that, when anyone opened the door to the chicken coop, he would lean his head forward to peer at them. If it was Grandma Minnie, he lowered his head and pecked with the hens.

In the garage, Mr. Covington had all kinds of mechanic's tools that interested me. Sometimes his buddies came by and indulged in "man talk," passed a bottle, smoked cigars and welded a bit, talking about cars, women and sports. When things got lively, somebody would remember to shoo me out. Usually, I hid close by so I wouldn't miss the good stuff. One day, I was sitting on a little wooden box with an oilcloth over it so I could watch Mr. Covington work. When the man talk started, Grandpa George said, "Leave that boy alone. He got to learn." It meant he thought I was old enough to be part of the conversation.

Grandma Minnie didn't trust the banks and kept her money at home. After she died, Aunt Elizabeth found $2,500 in bills under her mattress. She was so thrifty she would iron brown paper bags she got from the store and reuse them. Grandpa was quiet and reserved. He worked on the Pennsylvania Railroad as an oiler. A black man, Elijah McCoy, invented a system whereby machines could be oiled while in use that revolutionized industry, that's why "the real McCoy" became a synonym for anything authentic. Grandpa George was a master of the unspoken word. When Grandma Minnie would ask him something, he would answer with a sound, "Mm-hm." If something impressed him, he would add a syllable, "mm-mm-mm!" Like we say, "Damn!"

When people grew boastful, his favorite expression was "You don't say?" He never ever uttered God's name in vain. According to Uncle Wilbur, an inveterate bad boy, "When Papa beat me he'd say, 'Plague take him! Plague take him!' with each blow of the belt." Uncle Wilbur was the oldest of Grandpa George's five children. When Grandpa married Grandma Minnie, Wilbur was already twelve. He didn't take a shine to her. He decided to go to Belpre, Ohio to live with his Uncle Bradley, who worked as a bellhop in a hotel there. That's where he got his first job. He'd tell me about hotel life, the ladies of the night and their johns and how he developed his technique with the gangsters who frequented the hotel. When they checked in, he'd take their bags to their rooms, slip something into the door so it wouldn't close completely and linger in the hallway until he heard the water running in the shower. Then he'd slip back into the room and take a little something they wouldn't notice, a couple dollars or a pinch of cocaine. A natural rogue, he was a diligent student of human nature and relied on his instincts. He travelled with the circus as a roustabout because he was big and strong even as a lad. He was a hobo, a cowboy, a confidence man, a private detective, a bouncer in a cathouse and an occasional jail bird. Once, he got arrested for impersonating a cop. He joined the Navy because he liked to travel. He was a cook during WWII. One day the ship he was on came under attack and one of the gunners got killed. They ordered Wilbur to take his place. He was scared shitless but lived to tell the tale.

Mr. Cundiff was an old man whose skin looked like leather. He always wore a flat cap, denim pants with braces and chewed tobacco. He had a big wooden barn near our house where he kept his horse and wagon, a brass spittoon and bales of hay. He delivered ice to all the houses. I rode next to him as he made his deliveries so everybody in the neighborhood got to know me and I got to know them. They called me "Sonny Boy." I was energetic and curious about lot of things, willing to help anybody do anything. Some of the neighbors would call to my mother, "Bea! Bea! Is Sonny home?" They'd be in their yards or come by the house and ask Mama if I could run an errand for them. In those days, there were no prohibitions about what a child could purchase at a store. A lot of times they would wrap the money up in a handkerchief and I would take it to the store, along with a shopping list. If Mrs. Thompson wanted wine or cigarettes there was no problem handing them to a kid who everybody knew. This was before refrigerators became household items. Most people had a wooden icebox to keep things cold. There were no grocery stores where I grew up. People went directly to farmers to get their staples. Home delivery started with milkmen and bread men whose trucks went from house to house. Every home had a milk box where fresh milk was placed and empty bottles returned every day. The top quarter of the bottle was heavy cream and you had to shake it to blend it before you poured a glass. The milkman also delivered butter and eggs. The bread man delivered bread, rolls, and pastries directly to the door. There was also a man who sharpened knives and carried his pedal-powered grinding wheel on his back. He walked down the street ringing a bell so that everyone knew he was in the neighborhood. Sometimes, he had a little monkey on a string that did tricks to keep the kids amused while he sharpened their families' bladed implements. All that disappeared during and after the Second World War. Suddenly, everything was mechanized. You didn't have to take the rug outside and beat it with a triple-headed rug beater to get the dirt out if you had a Hoover vacuum cleaner in the house. Washing machines and refrigerators began to appear. People craved these conveniences and doled out their hard-earned pay in monthly installments with interest to acquire them. Near the top of everyone's list were electric fans and gramophones that played shellac records so you didn't have to wait for the radio to play your favorite tunes.

I went to kindergarten at Paxy's Playschool, run by Mrs. Paxton. Mr. Paxton picked us up in his big old Packard on days that were cold or rainy. The car could hold eight or nine kids. My first time on stage was at Paxy's. I played the Prince in Sleeping Beauty and had to sing a little song:

"I think you are sweet,
I'm anxious to meet
A beautiful lady like you.
I have come forth with
Love in my heart
Nothing can keep me from your side."

So saying, I brandished the cardboard sword hanging from my belt and kissed the princess on the cheek.

"Awake now to life, joyful and bright!"

She opened her eyes and offered me her hand. As we walked offstage our families cheered. I was sweet on Carol, the girl who played the princess. Mama bought me a pint of ice cream as a reward.

I remember my first day of first grade at Pilgrim Elementary School as if it were yesterday. Mama took me there. My teacher's name was Mrs. Jackson. She was very tall. Some of the kids were crying and hanging on to their mothers. They didn't want to let go. I was happy to wave goodbye. This was a new experience. Marvin Perkins, the boy who sat behind me, wept bitterly. His mother was ready to leave but, every time she moved toward the door, his wailing increased in volume. He and his mama lived right next to my grandparents on Harvard Street. It was the first time I realized that not everyone had two parents. If I misbehaved at school, Grandma heard about it first, she'd tell my aunt Kate who lived next door to us and then Kate would tell Mama. It's hard to get away with anything when your family is so tight-knit.

During the Second World War, my mother and father both worked at the Lockheed plant in Columbus, where they made fighter planes. They worked the night shift and when they came home they'd go straight to bed. We'd be getting ready to go to school. But before we'd leave the house, with Sissy as the look-out, I'd crawl on my knees into their room and go through his pants pockets or her pocketbook until I found some change that I knew they wouldn't miss. We'd buy a bagful of penny candy on the way to school.

One Sunday, at Union Grove Baptist Church, Reverend Hale was preaching about stealing, lying and the wages of sin. He looked right at my sister as he said, "... and you could burn in Hell!" She sat bolt upright, wide-eyed, quaking with fear. I was four years younger than Narcissia. Hell or no hell, we'd have plenty of candy. She confessed to my father one day when I was out delivering papers. By the time I got home, everybody was eating dinner. I was late because I went sliding on the ice with my friends. When I came in, I looked at Sissy. She was sniffling and looking down at her plate. I knew something was up. That's when my father glared at me. "Your sister told me that you've been stealing." He snatched me up out of that chair and into the bathroom before I could open my mouth. Shutting the door behind us, he told me to remove my shirt, tied my hands to the chair, took his leather razor strap and started to beat the snot out of me. I heard Mama pleading on the other side of the door, "Honey, don't kill him! That's your oldest son!" To which my father replied, "No son of mine is going to steal!" and continued to beat me. When he opened the door, my mother and sister ran in. My back was full of welts. My father returned to the table to finish his meal. My sister was sobbing, "I'm sorry, Adger Wilbur, I'm sorry!" as she applied salve to my wounds. My mother was very upset with my father. "Honey, you didn't have to beat him so hard." He repeated, "No son of mine is going to steal!" I never stole anything from anyone again.

The neighborhood I grew up in had all types of people. There was Mr. Lemons who ran the drugstore, Mr. Mullins who ran the Kroger corner grocery and Mr. Gram who ran the Shell gasoline station. My mother had rented the top floor of our house to Mr. and Mrs. Derwent. They were a "mixed couple." Next door to us were Mr. and Mrs. Logan. He worked in a factory and she was a beautician. Next door to the Logans were Mr. and Mrs. Lewis. They were always arguing and fighting. Their neighbors were Mr. and Mrs. Thompson. He would sit on the porch, reading the paper and drinking beer. Mrs. Thompson was always home. She was one of my favorite neighbors because she'd always have errands for me to do and she'd give me a little something when I completed them.

When Joe Louis won a fight, we would march around the neighborhood, banging on a big tin washing tub, led by a very pretty older girl. All the boys looked up to her. If you got out of line, she would grab you by the collar. There was a neighborhood wino whose name was Buster. He had seen action in WWII and always wore his long, green Army coat, regardless of the weather. He'd walk around talking to himself and waving his hands. People would find him asleep in their doorways and give his shoulder a shake, "Buster, get up and go home!" He had a wife who was always yelling at him and would smack him upside the head in public. Sometimes he'd have a black eye. But, when they came to church on Christmas Eve or Easter Sunday, she had him all cleaned up.

Across the street from our house a white couple lived on a small lot in a trailer. They were drinkers, too. They had two or three little kids running around. She would be in her house-dress and slippers. He wore a sleeveless undershirt and suspenders to keep his pants up over his belly. Most of the people in our neighborhood were factory workers. Superior Cleaners, my uncle James's business, was right next door to our house. He also owned the two houses on the other side of it. People were proud of the homes they owned, they kept their grass cut and their sidewalks swept.

One day, as we were having Sunday dinner, Mama asked me to go down to the basement and unplug the washing machine. I was still small so I had to stand on a milk crate in order to reach the plug. In those days, after the clothes were finished washing, they were put through the ringer to squeeze out excess water so they would dry faster on the clothesline. The ringer consisted of two rubber rollers. To pull myself up on the crate, I grabbed hold of the rollers without realizing the machine was still on. Before I knew it, my left hand was being pulled through the ringer.

"Mama! Mama!"

"Come upstairs, boy, there ain't no rats down there."

As my screams grew louder, Mama knew something was wrong. By the time she got to me, the rollers were grinding the skin off my left shoulder. Mama pulled the plug of the washing machine out of the socket and popped the latch on the rollers. They rushed me to Dr. Emanuel, who had gone to school with my mother. He applied some kind of purple salve to my arm and wrapped it with gauze from fingertips to shoulder. It took a long time to heal. My dog Foxy, who usually slept at the foot of the bed, would lie down right next to my wounded arm every night until the bandages were removed.

On Saturday afternoons, my sister and I would pull our wagon with two empty gallon containers to the Diamond Milk Bottling Company on Grandville Avenue, two blocks from our house. There they would refill them with buttermilk, one with flecks of butter and one plain, and we would bring them home. My mother would make a big pan of thick yellow cornbread that she would crush up in our bowls and pour the buttermilk over. My father liked the flecked buttermilk. Saturday was the time for family to appear at our door. I remember Aunt Dora and Uncle Charles at the table. He was a big, tall man who wore heavy shoes called brogans and didn't talk that much. He had a wicked scar that ran from his ear to the corner of his mouth. When I got older, it looked to me like a knife wound because most of the guys at that time carried knives. I asked my aunt Dora how he got it and she told me to ask him but I never did. Aunt Dora was a good-looking woman with chocolate-colored skin, sparkling eyes, naturally long eyelashes, a gold tooth and the sweetest voice. "Come over here, Adger Wilbur, and give your aunt a hug!" I was a cute kid with dimples on both cheeks. The women in my family made a big fuss over me. The perfumed warmth of their affection is a lasting memory. I grew up feeling very close to women. I still do.

I wanted to get out of the house and make some money so I became a paperboy. At first, I walked my route. I carried two different papers, The Citizen and the Dispatch. The Citizen was a morning paper. The Dispatch came out in the evening and had a special, Sunday edition. Sometimes, on stormy or snowy Sundays, my father drove my brother Harold and me around my delivery route. My customers came to appreciate me because they knew I cared about them. When it rained, I tucked the paper inside their screen door so it wouldn't get wet. I had always wanted a bike but we couldn't afford a new one. When Mr. Ross's son joined the Army, he sold his bike to my father. But I wasn't aware of that until the day of my fifteenth birthday. When I came home from school for lunch, my mother asked me to go out and get some eggs from the chicken coop.

"I'll get them this evening."

"You go out there right now and get those eggs!"

When I entered the coop, there was a beautiful black-and-cream-colored Schwinn 26-inch bicycle on its kickstand with a big red hen on the seat. Along with the thrill of having my first set of wheels, delivering papers on a bike increased my range and the number of customers I could serve.

I liked carrying papers because it got me out of the house and I met all kinds of people. There were customers who paid you on time and others who didn't. I began to understand how people were. Some gave me gifts at Christmas or invited me in for a glass of eggnog. My mother told me never to go into anyone's home or eat any food I was offered. I carried papers to three large apartment buildings. There was a black couple who worked as custodians for all three who always invited me in for a sandwich or a piece of cake. My customers liked me because they knew I cared about them. I had one of the biggest routes in the station: 108 customers. Bud Merritt, the station manager, proclaimed one evening that he would no longer accept change when we turned in our money. Since my route was so large I'd come back with my pockets full of change and no time to go to a store to change everything into dollars. One Saturday, as I emptied my pockets and began to count my change at the table, Bud Merritt said, "You're fired!"

That evening, as I delivered my route, I told some of my favorite customers that this was my last day. "Why?" Mrs. Schneider asked. I told her the reason and she said, "That doesn't make any sense." When I went home and told my mother I'd been fired, she had a similar response. Early Sunday morning, Bud Merritt appeared at our door. "Some of your customers called in and you got your route back." Mrs. Schneider was the organizer. She was a kind person and always gave me a big tip at Christmas. I won a trip for the Weekend Newspaper Boy Convention in Chicago because I got the most new customers. We stayed at the La Salle Hotel, attended a Black Hawks game, and went to the movies.

Mr. Hannan was the janitor at my grade school, Pilgrim Elementary, which had a big gym. On Saturdays, he opened it up for the junior high kids to play basketball. Mr. Hannan loved the game and always played on one of the teams. One Saturday, I was getting a lot of rebounds. He said, "Boy, you cleanin' them blackboards like Ajax!" The name stuck with me all the way through college. When I got to New York, Gordon Parks asked me if I had a nickname. I told him, "Ajax." He started to call me "Jax." Some people couldn't say or spell Adger correctly. So I stamped my first photos "Ajax." I still answer to that.

CHAPTER TWO

GOSPEL TRUTH

My grandparents were religious, lifelong members of Shiloh Baptist church. But when my father and mother married, they started to attend Union Grove Baptist, maybe because it was only a few blocks from home. Where we ended up going on any given Sunday depended on who the visiting preacher was. My favorite was Reverend Bentley, a towering, light brown, handsome man who, when moved by the fire of the Gospel, would step down off the pulpit and walk over the pews. People would part like the Red Sea to let him pass. He looked like a giant, holding the Bible in front of him like a cross so you knew it had a direct connection to spirit and everything heavenly. Mrs. Campbell, our organist, would launch into a spiritual and the choir's lead singer, Miss Carrie Parker, would rear back until I could see every tooth and celebrate the gospel with a soulful rendition of "Lord, I'm Comin' Home." The brothers and the sisters would be shouting and praising the Lord. My mother held her Bible like a precious jewel, saying, "Praise Him, Praise Him, Praise the Lord." My aunt Ida would put hers to the side, rise to her feet and shaking all over, saying, "Yes, Lord, Yes, Lord, Yes, Lord!"

Miss Lawson, a dignified spinster, would leap from her pew as if she had been struck by a bolt of holy lightning and start to gallop around the church. It would be up to the Deacons and the Eastern Star Sisters who cared for the sick and brought food to the poor, to head her off at the pass. Once they corralled her, they held her tight, put icepacks on her head and fanned her with the big church fan until she came to her senses. When I was eleven or twelve years old, Miss Lawson's Sunday morning gallivanting was both entertaining and instructive. I began to think I might enjoy being a preacher who could make the gospel move people like that. My cousin Ulysses Simpson Grant Bunche (who was called "Junior" because his father bore all the same names) and I had to contain our mirth at Miss Lawson's antics, especially since my father was sitting right behind us, poised to strike. As junior ushers we had to conduct ourselves like men when, at the end of the sermon, we put on white gloves to pass the shiny brass collection plates lined with red velvet down the aisles for the parishioners to make their Sunday donations. In the Baptist church this was known as "tithing." Each donation was supposed to represent a tenth of the donor's weekly income. Mama always put hers in a sealed envelope that tended to upset Daddy because he knew how much she cared about our church. She made a little money on the side with her pound cake and no one at the bake sales could resist her coconut brittle. But Daddy was the one who brought home the bacon. When he would ask, "Bea, how much did you put in the plate?" she would just smile.

Mama was the relief pianist at the church. Sometimes, I would play the trumpet and Mama would recite Alfred Joyce Kilmer's poem, "Trees." Another poet she admired was Paul Laurence Dunbar. Her favorite of his dialect verses was "Little Brown Baby." She would act it out. Some Sundays they would stand me on the Deacon's chair and I would recite from memory the names of the Books of the Bible, Old Testament and New, in front of the church. I was eight or nine years old at the time. After Sunday dinners, Mama brought out her photo albums. Some of them she had started as a little girl. She gathered us around her, opened the books and we could see her family when they were younger.

Her aunts and uncles, new babes in arms, my Uncle Wilbur's first girlfriend, Mama's first dog and cat, pictures of flowers my mother admired, wintertime pictures, changing seasons, picnics, weddings, family occasions of every sort. On days when it was raining or I was bored, I'd pull my mother's albums out and look at them. She must have had eight or nine books like that, filled with pictures. Each album contained four or five hundred pictures. They weren't just pictures she took, she collected other family members' photos as well. Everybody collected pictures back then. Kodak made America a picture-taking society because anyone could shoot a picture, anytime, anywhere, much like they use cell phone cameras today. I had an idyllic life as a young kid growing up in an extensive African American family. I never thought too much about the outside world. My brothers, sisters and I were always involved with each another. We listened to radio shows, read comic books, played games, enjoyed family get-togethers. There were no gangsters or drugs in our neighborhood. Ghetto life was unknown to me until I moved to New York City.

There was a half hour break between Sunday school and church. My cousin Earl lived across from Union Grove Baptist. He was one of the Tuskegee Airmen and had flown with General Benjamin O. Davis during the Second World War. When he was home on furlough, we would run over there and listen to his war stories. On other Sundays, Junior and I ran down a couple of blocks to Mount Vernon Avenue, which was the main drag with all the clubs and juke joints. We paid close attention to the way the young cats dressed. They wore zoot suits, pegged pants and alligator shoes. When they ambled down the street in all their finery, it was the essence of hip. One Sunday, Junior and I decided to emulate their strutting. We sashayed up the aisle hoisting the collection plates aloft. When we passed the family pew, my father reached out from his seat and slapped us both upside the head in front of the whole congregation. The little kids laughed, "tee hee hee." We were mortified because the girls saw us get slapped. We weren't bad boys. We just got carried away. We were taught to respect our elders. If you didn't, there'd be hell to pay.

Church was where I learned to smoke cigarettes. The custodian, Mr. Charles, would stoke the furnace with coal. Junior and I liked to hang out in the furnace room, especially when it was cold. We noticed that Mr. Charles kept his pack of Lucky Strikes on a ledge near the furnace. One day when we were alone down there we took one of his cigarettes, lit it up and starting coughing and choking on the smoke. Luckily, he never found out. We also enjoyed the after-service dinners. That's where the sisters would show off their culinary skills, trying to outdo each other. My aunt Ida's macaroni and cheese was always a big hit. My aunt Kate's coconut cake and my mother's pound cake always ran out first. The folks at the front of the line knew who had made what and would always point to the most popular items when it came their turn to be served.

Because my cousin and I were junior ushers, we helped count the money in the church office and, when that was done, we'd rush straight downstairs so we could be at the front of the line. When a lot of people came to church, which was always the case when Reverend Bentley was preaching, it took longer to count the money and, by the time we got downstairs, the food was gone. But I knew, once I got home, my mother would have hot buttered rolls, fried chicken, candied sweet potatoes, succotash and lemonade with mint I'd pick from the garden and she cut up to make the best lemonade in the world. My father was always at the head of the table at Sunday dinners. My mother would send my older sister Narcissia home a little early to put the rolls in the oven. Before we went to Sunday school, she rolled them out, shaped them and placed a damp towel over the pan so they would rise. Sissy would pop them in the oven so that, by the time we got home, they'd be ready to eat. My father was always served first. To his right were my mother, my younger brother Vincent, Sissy at the other end of the table, me to her right and my middle brother Harold next to my father. All the food was brought to the table straight from the stove and we would say the blessing. There was always a pile of chicken because we raised them in the back yard where my father had built a special coop. There were at least a hundred, sometimes a hundred and fifty chickens in the back yard. We didn't see red meat until after the War. Once in a while, my father came home with a piece of beef from the doctor's table wrapped in a napkin. He and Mama would eat that. Sometimes, attenuated family members joined us. Like aunt Ruby, not a blood relative but Mama's pal since grade school. She always said, "Bea, I want to come by and see the children." She would arrive, bearing what my father called a "two-by-four bit present." When the food was being served, Ruby always said, "My, it smells wonderful Bea but I have to go and leave you with your family." To which Mama invariably replied,

"Oh, Ruby, why don't you stay to dinner?"

"Oh, no, I didn't come for dinner, Bea."

"Ruby, just take your hat off and have a seat."

My father never interrupted their dialogue but we knew he didn't share Mama's regard for Ruby. Sometimes, when she made a peach cobbler, Ruby asked for a second helping. When it came time for her to leave, Mama would ask aunt Ruby if she wanted to take some food home. The way she treated Ruby was the way she treated everybody. Mama was generous to a fault.

On special holidays like Fourth of July and Thanksgiving, uncles and aunts came from near and far—Detroit, Chicago, South Carolina. The men filled big zinc washtubs with ice to put the watermelons in. The women spent hours in the kitchen, preparing a feast. My father was in charge of making peach, strawberry, and vanilla ice cream in a hand-cranked churn. You added ice and rock salt to keep it cold and churned away until the fruit and cream got nice and thick. I still remember the taste.

My uncles stood in the back yard, puffing cigarettes, cigars and pipes and indulging in "man talk." My mother wouldn't let anybody smoke in the house. "Keep those cigarettes outside, please!" She couldn't stand cigars. Unlike Aunt Liz who'd be passing out smokes to the fellows from her pack of Pall Malls and matching them tale for tale. She was younger than the other women, what Mama called "fast." She worked with her sisters in the kitchen but, every once in a while, she stopped what she was doing and headed for the back yard, still in her apron, to join the men for a drink, a joke and a smoke.

CHAPTER THREE

LIFE LESSONS

My sister was a top student. All her report cards had straight As. My mother was like that, too. I got a couple of As but mostly Bs and Cs. Sissy was my protector when I was in grade school. If someone picked on or bullied me she beat him up. She'd grab him by the ear like a dog and, by the time she'd let go, he'd be whimpering. She was born four years before me so, when she went to junior high, I had to learn how to fight. We had a yo-yo contest in school. Sissy won first place and I got second. My mother and father were proud of us. Sometimes our achievements were rewarded with a pint of Borden's ice cream. When we graduated from high school, my mother promised we would each get a watch. I got a Bulova with a black face. Bulova was the finest watchmaker in America then.

On special occasions, my cousin Neil drove to Columbus from Detroit, where he worked at the Ford factory. He was a tall man with light-brown skin and gray hair who always smoked a big cigar. He always appeared with a shiny new car. Neil was the one who taught me to ride a bicycle backwards. You'd sit on the handlebars, backwards. Instead of pushing down on the brakes, you'd push back. All the kids loved him because he told great stories.

I was an inquisitive kid and I liked learning new things. I read Scientific American and was interested in anything that was different than what we were taught at school. I had a little pocket microscope with which I loved to examine things "too small for the naked eye." Junior and I made walkie-talkies out of tin cans and wire. I had a pocketknife with all kinds of tools in it. We got to read all the best comic books because, when the doctor's kids got through with them, my father brought big boxes of them home. That's how Look and Life and National Geographic entered our lives. They opened a window to the world. The only publications we had family subscriptions to were Ebony and Jet. My parents made sure we were all members of the NAACP.

Without Sissy to defend me, I was a reluctant combatant. I used my speed to avoid getting hurt. If I were threatened, I would run to my aunt Kate's house because it was close to the school. I relied on her being there to open the door. One day, with a gang of boys at my heels, I ran up on her porch. She saw me coming and slammed the door shut. In a panic, the only thing I could think of was to pick up one end of her heavy porch swing and tip it in the direction of my pursuers. As it banged its way down the wooden steps, they leaped out of the way, yelling "That boy's crazy!" and shaking their heads. A few days later, they asked me to join their gang. I realized that, under pressure, I had a little demon inside of me that would serve me well in circumstances I could not control. I wasn't the kind of kid who went around picking fights and hurting people but, when threatened, I reacted spontaneously in a way that got me out of the mess.

My mother, my sister and I were members of the Houston Players, named after Mrs. Houston, the company's director. We traveled the church circuit, dramatizing Bible stories. Our repertoire included a Christmas play, Daniel in the Lion's Den, the story of Saul who became Saint Paul and spread the word of Jesus. Our musical director was Jack's mother. Jack rented the small house that my uncle James owned next door to ours that he made into an artist's studio. He would let me hang out as he worked and I found it fascinating that someone could pick up a pencil and draw a picture of something I would instantly recognize. His mother was equally talented. She would whistle in a variety of styles and melodies to accompany Mrs. Houston at the piano. My mother, sister and I were three actors in a company of ten. We would travel in a caravan of cars, bearing our sets, costumes, and lighting equipment to different churches as far away as Akron, Dayton and Chillicothe. When I was small, I played the part of Baby Jesus. One of the actors would lead me onstage by the hand. My head would be wrapped in a colorful cloth turban and I wore a little white robe. As I got older, I became one of the shepherds in the field. Our silhouettes were projected on a backdrop by a low-angled spotlight. In retrospect, I realize that my photographer's eye was being trained from the start.

Mr. Ward was the director of our choir. He was a handsome, dark-complexioned man with shiny skin and beautiful teeth who had a very deep voice. When he sang "Deep River," he sounded like Paul Robeson. Bobby and Hysel Taylor, Cleveland Parker and I formed a quartet called "The Wardneers" in his honor. By this time, I was in high school. We traveled a similar circuit to that of the Houston Players. I played accompaniment on a baritone ukulele. Otherwise we were strictly a capella, with me singing bass. I was already playing trumpet in the school band and orchestra and taking lessons from Dr. Freitag at Capital University in Bexley, Ohio. I had musical ambitions. But the baritone ukulele I learned from a book. The Wardneers were very popular. I was part of another a capella quartet called "The Heartbeats" who sang popular songs of the day, led by Johnny Johnson, a pretty yellow brother with a Jackie Wilson voice who drove the girls mad. We were ready to record, waiting for a contract from Detroit. When I graduated from East High, I was offered a full scholarship to study music at Capital University. But there were conditions: they wanted me to go back to high school for one semester and improve my grades in math and English. I talked with my English teacher who said, "This would be a great opportunity. Don't miss it." But I was depressed at the thought of returning to high school. I had done enough to graduate, but not to excel. That summer, my mother said she didn't want me sitting around the house all day, drawing and making imitation Calder mobiles out of pieces of wood and sticks I found in the back yard. At night, I slipped out of the house, attracted to the nightlife on Mount Vernon Avenue. I had a girlfriend, Jane Pace, who was a great piano player and I took her to her gigs in my father's Dodge and brought her back to her house afterwards. There were a lot of up-and-coming musicians around Columbus at the time. I remember seeing the blind reedman Roland Kirk at Skirtie's Music Bar when we were both still in high school. He was already making a name for himself because he could play two saxophones at once. I had aspirations to be a professional musician.

One day, my sister's boyfriend left a photography magazine at our house. I picked it up and leafed through it. I came across an announcement: "Ohio University Gives Degree in Photography."

"Look, Mom, I can get a college degree in photography."

"Really?"

As an amateur photographer, she was immediately partial to my cause.

"You realize we have to show this to your father."

When I told him the news, he shook his head, "Why do you need a college degree to take pictures? That's nonsense! Eastman Kodak sends you a camera with the film already in it. You take pictures, send the camera back to them and they send you both the pictures and the camera back, loaded with a fresh roll of film. You'd better get something worthwhile in your head, boy." My mother turned her sweetest smile on him: "But, honey, that's what he wants to do." When she turned on her charm, she was irresistible.

I entered Ohio University in September of 1954. I was on the road to what my parents desired for all their children—a college degree. But, like most of my classmates, I partied for the first two years. Even so, all my grades in the photography courses were good. I was happy to be away from home. Ohio University was seventy-five miles from Columbus. At that time, the only other school in the country that offered a degree in photography did not admit "negroes." I had discovered my craft.

I told myself, "I can get a college degree and get my parents off my case." I had a buddy named Roosevelt Carter who was a newspaper stringer. He rode around in his car at all hours, monitoring police reports. When he found out that I was interested in photography, Roosevelt invited me to ride along. With the short wave as his guide, he would rush to the site, take pictures and sell them to different news outlets. He was usually first on the scene because he was already in his car, waiting for something to happen. One day, Roosevelt said, "My camera club is going to do a photo shoot. Would you like to come along?"

That Saturday, there was a Shriner's Day Parade in Columbus. We went to a basement studio with a white, no-seam background hung up. Soon after we arrived, someone announced the session was starting. I looked around and saw a woman sitting in a chair with a robe on. She got up, untied the robe and let it drop to the floor. I had never seen a naked woman up close. I didn't take one picture. I was sweating profusely and told Roosevelt I had to go home. I went upstairs and watched the parade. After the session, Roosevelt came up to me and said, "That was the first time you ever saw a naked woman?" "Yup." I was sixteen years old.

I got my first camera by signing my father's name, Adger W. Cowans, which was the same as mine. They didn't do credit checks back then or they would have known his middle name was Watson and mine was Wilbur. If you had a job, you qualified to pay for purchases "on installment." When they delivered the camera together with a Magnavox high fidelity record player, my father went berserk. He wasn't rich. In fact, we were poor. I was a senior in high school and still had my paper route. So I promised him I would pay him back over time. He looked me straight the eye.

"You ain't never going to make that kind of money taking pictures."

"I promise I'll pay you back."

That Christmas, I got $80 in tips from the hundred-some-odd customers on my two paper routes. I gave $40 to my father. But what really blew his mind was, years later, when I had my first job in New York. I went home one weekend to see him when he was in the hospital, and handed him $250 cash. He looked at the money, then he looked at me.

"Where'd you get this money?"

"From taking pictures."

He shook his head in wonder: "Mm-mm-mm!" I could sense his pride in me. That was the last time I saw him alive.

When I was at Ohio University and studying photography I wanted a Leica because that was the camera that all the bad cats I liked were using, W. Eugene Smith, Henri Cartier-Bresson, and Robert Capa. But I didn't have the money. I was using a Rolleicord that I liked but it wasn't a camera with which you could shoot spontaneously and I didn't care much for the square format. When I told my Aunt Elizabeth I wanted a Leica, she asked how much it cost. "Three hundred dollars." It was just before Christmas. She said, "Let me think about it." A couple days later, she called and said, "I'll do it but consider it your present for the whole year." I received an envelope with three crisp one hundred dollar bills that week. I gave them to my classmate, Taber Chadwick, who told me about the deal. When I got back to campus after Christmas break, he handed me a red leather box with a brand new Leica M-2 inside. I went crazy. I took pictures of everything I saw. The Leica was like an extension of my eye. It reminded me of when I got my first camera and thought, if I slept with it under my pillow, I could wake up fast enough to photograph my dreams. For any photographer who was serious, a Leica was a must.

I was always an avid collector of long-playing records (LPs), unbreakable discs twelve inches in diameter that spun on your turntable at thirty-three and a third revolutions per minute. In those days, you could buy new LPs for under $5. I was mostly into jazz although I also liked classical composers like Mozart, Beethoven and Brahms. Chopin, Debussy, and John Phillip Sousa were familiar to me from the high school orchestra. But jazz was my religion. I listened to the founders of bebop, Miles Davis, Charlie Parker, Dizzy Gillespie and Thelonious Monk, appreciated the big band sounds of Duke Ellington and Count Basie and was a big fan of the Modern Jazz Quartet with John Lewis on piano, Percy Heath on bass, Connie Kay on drums and Milt Jackson, the incredible "Bags," on vibraphone.

Our sculpture teacher, David Hostetler, was a drummer and jazz fanatic. On weekends, when Miles was at Carnegie Hall or Monk was at the Five Spot, Miss E.J. Tracey, Jim Dine, Charley Heald, Miss Chris Arndt and myself would pile into David's car and head for Manhattan. We would go to clubs and attend concerts on Friday and Saturday and drive back to school in time for our Monday morning class, still filled with the excitement of having seen the jazz masters live. What a thrill it was to bask in the heat of their ceaseless creation! We were such regulars that, one weekend, at The Five Spot, Monk himself approached,

"Ain't you them kids from that school in Ohio?"

"Yeah!"

He went over to the piano and played a few chords.

"That's for y'all."

We were thrilled. We couldn't believe we had been noticed, let alone recognized, by one of our idols.

When Chris Arndt moved to East 53rd Street to work in New York we slept on her floor on blankets or in sleeping bags. If she wasn't around, we slept in the car. Sometimes, we stayed at Wally Uno's apartment in the same building as Chris. We called him Wally One—he was a jazz maniac like the rest of us. Years later, I wrote a poem in honor of my jazz heroes as part of the first Water show I did at The Greene Street Gallery. I called the show "Moments" and acknowledged the indelible link between music and image in my work.

When we came to Manhattan on those music-loving weekends, sometimes I had the chance to go to the Museum of Modern Art, which was less than a mile west of where we stayed on 53rd Street, as well as other museums and galleries. The action and life of the city inspired me. I loved walking the streets. My camera was always part of my outfit but I usually kept it hidden under my shirt or jacket. I was mainly a stealth shooter in those days. I had finally realized, in my junior year, that a picture was worth a thousand words. I found I could learn something about people by the way they responded to a photographic image I had taken. This led me to a greater understanding of the true meaning of art and how it can change one's perception of life. But the idea of being an artist was still foreign to me. I was more interested in becoming a good photographer. That title seemed honor enough—I didn't have to be an "artist." It was only when I began to understand that art was something that moved and transformed people that my self-perception shifted and grew. I became critical, not only of what I was "shooting," but of anything and everything that had to do with visual stimulation: fashion, dance, poetry, painting, music, film and theater. I read all of Da Vinci's notebooks and Kandinsky's writings about art. His theory about musical notes having colors fascinated me. I had never studied painting in school and I started to understand that it was emotional as well as visual. As Paul Klee wrote in his Pedagogical Sketchbook, "Art does not reproduce the visual, but makes visual." I began to understand what that meant. Eyes only see. It's the heart that feels.

As a child I can remember seeing things that other people didn't see. Two people can speak about something they've witnessed together but it's a different experience for each of them and they describe it differently. It's the same when I show my work—two people can see the same thing visually and respond to it in totally different ways. So when somebody understands and relates emotionally to something I have created I am elated because my work is the doorway to my spirit. It comes full circle. Someone relates to an image you have created in a way that you can relate to. You both agree that it's a beautiful nude, a beautiful sunset, beautiful music, even though your definition of beauty may be completely different.

The beauty of traveling was instilled in me at a very young age. I remember being in my grandfather's car on our way to see my uncle Wilbur in Cleveland. Sometimes I would get to sit in the front seat between grandpa and grandma. However, most times, I was in the backseat with Sissy and Harold, with the youngest sibling at the time, Vincent, sitting on my mother's lap. In those early days, African American people were not served in restaurants so we always brought food. We'd stop by the side of the road and my mother would spread out a tablecloth and serve us fried chicken, potato salad, green beans and macaroni. Mama called it "a picnic." It wasn't until I was older that I understood that we had no other choice. I would hear grandpa talking about "peckerwood this" and "peckerwood that" but I was a kid and didn't understand what he was talking about. I knew that something called "white trash" was found in trailers because sometimes it was referred to as "trailer trash."

After eating, we'd pack up the picnic basket, get back in the car and keep on rolling. One time we stopped by the side of the road and before Mama could put the food out, a white man with a shotgun came out of the woods and said, "You niggers get off my land!" That was one of the first times I remember being fearful because the man seemed angry and didn't look like anybody I'd ever met. My grandfather immediately stepped in front of the family while my mother gathered everything up and put it in the trunk. Grandma Minnie said, "Come on, George Watson, let's go." My father wasn't present because he was always working at the Doctor's place. In those days our family went everywhere by car: Detroit, Cleveland, Philadelphia, South Carolina. We even drove to New York. For me, as a little boy, traveling was heaven because I learned new things and I got to see the countryside, the trees, the animals, the people, all kinds of new stuff. I was a big daydreamer. I remember my mother coming to school to talk to my teacher, Miss Tyree, who was a dark chocolate colored woman with velvety skin and a beautiful mouth. She told my mother I was a good student but, when she called on me, she would often have to repeat my name because I would be lost in a daydream. From my present vantage point, it seems that what was called "daydreaming" has a lot to do with a fertile imagination. I realize now that my childhood was idyllic. I lived in a very protected world surrounded by a loving family. I saw my mother and father every day.

But, by the time I was fifteen years old, I was sick and tired of family. I felt so constricted. I wanted get up and go somewhere. I was ready to experience life on my own. I wanted to be able to sleep as long as I wanted, to eat what I wanted to eat. I could not wait to make decisions based on my own desires. When I felt that way, I would always call my grandpa and grandma and ask when they were going to D.C. Sometimes, aunt Kate's four sisters would come to visit us from down south. They were astonishingly beautiful, each one a different color. Mildred, my favorite, had dark skin and curly black hair and she would bring the latest records. That's when I first heard Louis Jordan's "Saturday Night Fish Fry" and "Big Fat Mama," which is still one of my favorites—I learned all the words and sang it constantly. I also loved Duke Ellington's "Tuxedo Junction" and Count Basie's "One O'Clock Jump." Mildred would take me by the hand to the corner store and buy me ice cream, hug me and sit so close to me I could smell her gorgeous perfume. I sure did love sitting next to Mildred—she was big and tall and as sweet as pie. It was exciting when they all stayed at uncle James's big house, a couple of doors down from ours.

I always loved going to see my Aunt Kate. As a matter of fact, I remember a time before I could walk when I crawled out the back door and through the fence that separated our two houses with an empty can of Gerber's baby food in my hand. I banged on her kitchen screen door with the can, she heard it but, when she looked out, she didn't see anybody. Finally, she looked down and there I was. She couldn't believe I had crawled all that way. Years later when I was coming cross country on my motorcycle, I stopped in Columbus and my Aunt Kate said, "Let me show you something." She still had that Gerber can. She told me she had been cutting her biscuit dough with it ever since the day I brought it to her door forty years before. Aunt Kate's husband, my father's youngest brother uncle James, had a cleaning and pressing business called Superior Cleaners next door to our house. One winter morning about 2 a.m., we were awakened by Aunt Kate banging on the door. She was shouting, "The shop is on fire and he's gone in there to get the books. Wake the children up! Your house is next." Thankfully, the firemen came and put out the fire before it spread. Uncle James's arms were singed but he had rescued the books. He kept a list of people who had paid for their clothes to be cleaned. Uncle James sent the clothes to a cleaning house where they were steamed and pressed before they were sent back. Since the books were intact and legible despite the fire, none of his customers could claim he owed them something that wasn't recorded. That was why he risked his life to get them. However, it didn't prevent some people from cooking up false claims.

Uncle James's and Aunt Kate's backyard was always well kept. They had a small garden, a grape vine, a pear tree and an apple tree. He always had a brand new car and wore nice suits to church. He owned three parcels of land on our block and had a successful business. James was very respected in our part of town. People came from all around to have their clothes cleaned because he was an honest man. He let customers know in advance that certain stains could not be removed. Everyone who knew him, trusted him. He worked long hours and had multiple racks of clothes, one above the other. He made a long stick with a v-shaped notch on the end. With it, he could latch onto the hangers and bring down clothes from racks that were beyond his reach. I worked for him during the summer and when I was at college I brought my clothes to the shop to be cleaned. He made me press them when they came from the dry cleaner's, something he had taught me to do.

One summer, Uncle James bought a new Buick Roadster with "Dynaflow" transmission and took me and Junior along on a trip home to South Carolina since we had both gotten our licenses and could help him with the driving. When it was my turn to drive, he stretched out on the backseat and went to sleep. Of course, I wanted to see how fast the car would go. When I got to 60 mph, I stomped on the gas pedal and the car shifted into high gear with a jolt. My uncle woke up immediately and started shouting, "Boy, slow the car down! Where do you think you're going?" He knew that colored drivers in the south were much more likely to be stopped by white patrolmen. Sure enough, a couple of hours later, with James at the wheel, we got stopped. He got out of the car and opened the trunk for the police. When he drove down south, my uncle always kept a double-barreled shotgun hidden in the trunk of his car. Aunt Kate, sitting inside the car with Junior and me, got very nervous: "Oh Lord, I hope James don't have to put his hands on that gun!"

Luckily, he didn't and we reached my Uncle Dewett's and Aunt Magnolia's house without further incident. The house my father was raised in was on stilts and made of logs with mud and newspapers stuck in the cracks between them. There was no electricity. When it got dark in the evening, they would light what they called "wind lanterns," kerosene lamps. There was a hearth with a fire where they heated water and cooked everything in big iron pots. The pots were hung on an iron bar that swung out over the fire. We bathed in a galvanized tub with water heated on the hearth. The little kids would bathe first, then the older kids would use the same water. When fresh water was heated for the adults, the men bathed first. There were no windows in the house, just wooden shutters. There was a mule, a cow, pigs and chickens, and a meat house where they usually had a side of beef or bacon curing. It was the first time that I used an outhouse. As a city boy, I saw it as an adventure. Junior and I had fun. In the morning, my cousin James took us out into the field and we busted open a big watermelon with a rock and then went swimming in the creek. It was the sweetest watermelon I'd ever tasted, bright red with big black seeds. My grandfather was a "freedman." I don't know how he acquired the land but there was a lot of it. He grew peanuts, okra, watermelon, green beans, corn, strawberries, tomatoes, potatoes, and yams in the rich red soil.

CHAPTER FOUR

AS I PICTURED IT

The first thing that amazed me about New York City was that it seemed that life was going on around the clock. One of my first discoveries was the Automat on West 57th Street, not too far from Carnegie Hall. It was a gigantic room with restaurant seating but, instead of menus and servers, the walls bore matrices of windowed compartments with different foods on plates behind them: hotdogs, hamburgers, various sandwiches, rice pudding, cream pies and the like. When you put the required number of coins in the slot, the window opened and you took out the plate. The streets were crowded with people, day and night, and the energy of multitudes of bodies in close proximity was like nothing I had ever felt. Visiting "the Big Apple," as the jazzmen called it, has always stimulated my imagination and hunger for experience. To be part of the throng, a straphanger on buses and subways, a ceaseless walker dodging taxis, a jazz nut listening to "Symphony Sid" on WEVD, going to the Five Spot, the Half Note, Birdland or the Village Vanguard anytime I liked, sitting at the bar and seeing the high priests and priestesses work their magic is a gift I will never take for granted. In those days, the subway was inexpensive and trains ran reliably in many directions, above and below street level. The riders were actors in the nonstop drama of human existence. It was one of my favorite places to photograph.

In Manhattan, art is everywhere, from the fashion tableaux in department store windows to the Old Masters, mummies and sarcophagi at the Metropolitan Museum and the Rodin, Giacometti, and Picasso pieces in the sculpture garden of the Museum of Modern Art. There are a lot of great cities in the world and, over the years, I have lived and worked in quite a few of them. But "the Apple" is my destiny, my spirit enlivener.

When I was a kid, we drove from Columbus, Ohio to the Bronx to see Aunt Thelma and Uncle Brad. On Easter Sunday, we cruised along 125th Street, ogling the sidewalks full of people in their Easter outfits. I'd never seen so many beautiful black people in one place.

In the Navy, when I was stationed at Oceana Naval Air Station in Virginia Beach, my aunt Elizabeth would call me from time to time.

"What you doing, kid?"

"Nothing special, aunt Liz. I'm bored stiff."

"You want to go to New York this weekend?"

"Yeah!"

I would take the Greyhound from Norfolk to D.C. and she'd be at the bus station, at the wheel of her brand new Pontiac, waving and calling my name. It didn't matter to her what time it was. To get to "the Apple" by daybreak, we spelled each other at the wheel, zipping north on U.S. 1. Aunt Liz's married name was Elizabeth Virginia Hall. She was a real character. She kept up with the latest fashions and always wore silk scarves, tailored suits, fox stoles, elegant shoes and hosiery. She carried leather gloves and pocketbooks. She was every inch beautiful. Whenever we kids were dissatisfied with things at home, we'd go to stay with aunt Liz in D.C. She was like our second mother. When the Polaroid Land Camera first hit the marketplace, she bought one and brought it back to Columbus. We loved to peel back the image and watch as it developed. Years later, when Polaroid launched the XS-70, I started to experiment with long exposures.

I invented a "bypass instrument" that would allow the shutter to remain open while I painted images with penlights and other lights and filters in the dark. When I was finished, I withdrew the instrument and allowed the image to develop. I created a series called "The Morning of the Blue Queen" with my friend Earlene as the Queen.

Another Christmas, Liz brought Sissy and me a little 8mm projector that played a Mickey and Minnie Mouse cartoon. Liz started her career as a secretary working for the Federal Government and was soon promoted to executive secretary. She worked for the Kennedy Administration and had a framed picture of President John F. Kennedy that he signed "to Virginia." Liz's gaiety was irrepressible, she loved to mess with strangers. She'd pull up alongside little imported cars, VWs, MGs and Austins, lower the Pontiac's automatic window and say, "Where you goin' with that little lemon squeezer?" She'd talk to strangers as if they were people she knew. We were driving down Lennox Avenue early one Easter morning when we saw a young woman staggering down the street in spike heels. Liz made a U-turn, rolled down the window and yelled, "Hey, girl, I know them shoes are killin' your feet!" The girl nodded and waved and my aunt sped away. She was the archetype of a "liberated woman" decades before that concept came into focus for me.

Her third and final marriage, to a man I called Uncle Tommy, was the one that stuck. Uncle Tommy's daddy was a sheriff from out west somewhere. Uncle Tommy impressed me from the moment I met him. He had a big moustache and wore Stetson hats. He and Aunt Liz had a small farm in Virginia where they kept riding horses. They also liked to hunt. Uncle Tommy worked as an inspector on the Pennsylvania Railroad. He had a quiet, kind strength. You knew right away he was a serious, responsible man.

On one of my visits, they decided I should learn how to ride. In D.C. there's a place where you can rent horses by the hour. We all rented horses, together with a bunch of their friends. The guy who ran the place helped me up on my steed.

"He's a good horse. He knows the trail. You won't get lost."

As soon as I got up on his back, the horse turned his head around, gave me the once over and took off like a bat out of hell. All I could go was hang onto the reins. We went galloping past other riders, including my aunt and uncle and their riding buddies. I smiled a frozen smile in their direction, shaking with adrenaline. They all seemed pleased with my progress, calling out encouragement: "Ride 'em, cowboy! High-ho Silver, away!"

The dumb ass horse was trying to kill me. He ran under a thick tree branch that, if I hadn't ducked, would have knocked me cold. That crazy horse ran the whole course and went straight back to the barn, panting. When I got off his back, he looked at me with disdain. The TV show "Mr. Ed" had made talking horses all the rage. I could hear him thinking, "You damn fool. You don't know how to ride!"

No one tried to rescue me. They thought I was a natural horseman. I told them "I'm never going riding again." Uncle Tommy laughed his ass off.

When I left Ohio University in 1958, I went back to Columbus. My mother asked me what I was going to do next. My uncle James advised me to find out if there were any black photographers. I didn't know of any so I asked my photography teacher, Walter B. Allen, who was from New York, if such people existed. He said, "I think there's a guy at LIFE." He couldn't remember his name. Researching, I came across a publication called LIFE Magazine Photographers. Gordon Park's picture was the only brown face in that group. I decided to write him a letter, in care of LIFE. I got a quick reply, "Look me up when you come to New York." That summer, when I was in town on one of Professor Hostetler's jazz junkets, Gordon and I met. He drove up in a glistening Thunderbird convertible, looking like a star. When I graduated in 1958, I returned to NYC and paid for a room at the 34th Street YMCA. When I phoned Gordon, he asked "Where you staying?" When I told him he said, "Pack up your stuff and come up to our house." I took a train to White Plains. Mr. and Mrs. Parks and their sons Gordon Jr., David, and Tony welcomed me like family. GP looked through my portfolio and asked what I wanted to do. When I told him I was uncertain, he said, "You can live here with us and come to work with me at LIFE." I worked and lived with Gordon and his family most of that summer. One day my mother called and told me I had a letter from the White House.

"Open it up and read it, Mama!"

"It says, 'Greetings from the White House. You have been selected among the fortunate few to serve in the Armed Forces of the United States of America.'"

I had already joined the Navy Reserves and I knew I was supposed to report for active duty when I was through with college. But I did not intend to pass up the chance to go to New York and work with the most famous black photographer in the world. Fate finally caught up with me. I returned to Columbus to see my Commanding Officer and pleaded with him to allow me to do active duty in the Navy instead of the Army. He said, "Okay, if you enlist right away." The only thing I had were the clothes on my back, my camera, and a little suitcase. Everything else I left in the apartment that Gordon, Jr. and I shared on 82nd Street. To make extra money, we played our guitars in the little cafés around Columbia University. Gordon had studied classical and flamenco guitar with Carlos Montoya. He was great looking and the way he presented himself to the world was catnip to chicks. I played backup guitar and sang harmony. We'd play a few songs, pass the hat and move on to the next place. Since we were more or less the same age as our audience, everyone figured we were Columbia undergrads so we were able to dispense with managers and contracts.

I came back to New York after I got out of the Navy in 1960. I had married Barbara Chavous, my high school sweetheart. We lived on Convent Avenue and 150th Street, sharing an eight-room apartment with other people. Barbara was teaching at a public elementary school in Harlem while I wandered the streets with my Leica. Then we moved to West 87th Street. Gordon Parks, Jr. had gotten married to an Armenian woman named Ziggy and they lived in the ground floor apartment. Barbara and I lived on the third floor. Hanging out together was a ball because we all got along. On the weekends, we went to the coffee shop at the 92nd Street Y where they had poetry readings and live music.

One weekend, Gordon and I are at his place with our friends, Johnny Guitar and Raimundo. The telephone rings, Gordon answers it,

"My friend Howie is coming with his car to take us over to the Y."

A half hour later, Howie's downstairs. We get in the car and cross Central Park at 86th Street when Howie decides to show off. He takes a left on two wheels going uptown on Fifth Avenue and the transit cops pull us over. They order us to come out of the car with our hands in the air and pat us down. No contraband. As they're frisking us, the unoccupied car is slowly rolling down the street. One cop tells the other to stop it and back it up to where we are. After a few minutes, he comes back and tells his partner,

"Cuff them! This car's hot. There's no key."

They take us to the 79th Street Precinct and lock us up. Two African Americans, one Puerto Rican, a blond Hawaiian kid carrying a guitar, and Howie, a skinny, wild-eyed Jewish kid nobody has ever seen before but Gordon. We're too hungry to be scared. When we tell them we have money and ask if they'll bring us sandwiches and sodas, the guys at the precinct are glad to oblige. One even has a list and writes down our orders. We're relieved. We have no idea why we're in jail. When we start to pressure him, Howie makes a spontaneous confession to anyone who will listen:

"They didn't know it was stolen. Let them go."

But the cops have us pegged as gang members. We're all in one cell. They tell us we can each make a phone call. Gordon calls Ziggy and tells her to call his dad. Johnny Guitar calls Hawaii. His father is rich. Raimundo lives by himself, no one to call. I call Barbara. It's now around midnight. We were supposed to meet her and Ziggy at the Y at 9.

"Barbara, you'll never guess where I am."

"You're right, I won't." Click. She's pissed.

They won't let me make another call. When we ask about the food, they say, "What food?"

"Man, we gave you money and you took our orders."

"Shut up!"

We spend the night in jail. Turns out that Howie has escaped from an upstate mental institution and stolen the car. He keeps apologizing, mostly to Gordon. We want to kick his ass but this is not the place. They put us in a paddy wagon and take us to Long Island City Prison where they confiscate all our belongings, strip search us, issue us numbers and prison garb without belts, separate us and lock us in cells. I get locked in with a madman. When they push me in, he is cowering in a corner. He never says a word, points to the top bunk. I lie down, my heart racing. "How'd I end up here?" I know I'm innocent. But being locked up is a drag. That night, my cellmate attempts to hang himself. I wake up to the sound of gagging. When I open my eyes, his face is turning purple inches from mine. The guards come in, cut him down, smack him a few times and throw him back in the cell. The next morning, I hear Gordon calling my name,

"Jax! Pops is coming to get me. I'll tell Barbara, Jax, where you are."

I'm disappointed. I thought Gordon, Sr. would get me out as well. I spend four more days in jail. Barbara has to call around to make my bail. She comes to get me in a beautiful dress. The bailiff sees we're poor. He intimates that, if Barbara favors him, he'll forgo the bail. We're incensed. Outside, we embrace. Barbara apologizes for having hung up on me. She's in tears. An elevated train rattles by like a chariot in the afternoon sun and I weep, too, happy to be free again.

Every now and then I landed a photographer assistant's job. I worked with Lillian Bassman, Henri Clark, Ben Somoroff, and Roy Calhoun, among others. When I first got to town, I met Morris Gordon who worked for Western Electric. He bought one of my photographs and encouraged me. Some years later, he submitted my name to speak at a photography conclave of some of the top professionals in Coral Gables, including some of the staff photographers from LIFE magazine. Jerry Uelsmann and I were "young lions" as yet untainted by commercialism. I showed slides of some of my images of water and Jerry did the same with his stuff. Our images left the guys from LIFE cold. Jerry was the first pre-digital photographer who manipulated images. When our presentations concluded, there were no questions. Later on, one of the old guard photographers asked, "You young guys got anything to say?" I said, "Everything is image" and sat back down. Jerry said, "I agree with Adger." No one offered us any feedback after that. Later that evening, Gordon Parks showed up and they made a big fuss over him. He came over to me and said, "Good to see you here, Jax!"

At that time, photography dealt mainly with documentation. There was no precedent for abstract pictures of water. After my presentation, I was sitting in my car when my agent came over and asked if I was okay. I told her I was. Then Ken Heyman, who had traveled the world and collaborated on a big book with anthropologist Margaret Mead, told me he thought my photographs were terrific.

"These guys are never going to understand the kind of work you and Jerry are doing. All they care about is making money."

He offered me the use of his dark room whenever I needed to make prints. It was on Park Avenue in the Fifties and very well-equipped. I gratefully accepted. In spite of a cool reception by the professionals, my trip to Coral Gables was turning out well.

There was a man from Amsterdam at the Florida gathering who published a magazine called Avenue and invited me to come to the Netherlands and shoot whatever I wanted to. My agent, Flora Kaplan, went with me. We traveled all over the place and I ended up taking a lot of photographs. Avenue published twelve pages of my work. I went to Amsterdam, Rotterdam, all the dams. I loved the windmills and the tulip fields. The light was incredible. I took one of my favorite water photographs standing on a bridge over one of the canals. My agent was starting to book a lot of travel work. Clay Felker, the founder of New York magazine, also gave me assignments from time to time. He was a tough negotiator and very direct. He liked my work and didn't care what color I was. I shot for Con Edison, the U.S. Army, some of the first ads for L&M cigarettes, and personality portraits for Pageant magazine—quite a bit of commercial work. I rented a studio on Union Square. But the world of commercial photography was not my bag. I wanted to shoot my own stuff.

Esquire magazine sent me to Brazil to shoot the revolutionary vanguard of underground filmmakers. When I got to Rio, the guy from Esquire who was supposed to give me an advance for my hotel and expenses, told me he was going to keep the money and stay in Brazil. I could see why—the women were beautiful and very receptive. Roz, a friend from New York, decided she was going to come with me. She had some money so we stayed at the Copacabana Palace Hotel. Because the black power movement was in the news then, a lot of Brazilians mistook us for Stokely Carmichael and Miriam Makeba. "Black power! Black power!" they shouted, raising their fists as we passed on the mosaic sidewalks of Avenida Atlântica. We ended up on local television, talking about what was happening in the U.S. in the fateful year of 1968. One day when I was napping, Roz came in the room and said, "Guess who's down by the pool in a big straw hat? Mick Jagger." I could not have cared less. "You mean you're not going to come down and talk with him?" I rolled over and went back to sleep. When I awoke, I went down and met him. He seemed like a very nice guy. He'd never been to Brazil before. He was there because he'd gotten into a bit of a tight spot in London and needed to chill. His girlfriend, Marianne Faithful, came with him and brought her young son, Nicholas. We went everywhere together, enjoying the sights and sounds of Rio. Cariocas, as natives of Rio are called, sang its praises as the marvelous city (cidade maravilhosa), which was easy to understand if you were living by the beach. When we told Mick and Marianne we were flying north to Bahia, they said they were headed there as well and suggested we take the same plane. As we left the hotel for Galeão airport, we drove under a double rainbow. We agreed that was a good omen. When we got to Salvador, the capital of Bahia, we dropped Mick and Marianne at their hotel. As we were about leave, Mick came running out: "They didn't get our reservation and they say they don't have any room!" Roz said that her husband had a house on Itapoã Beach where they could stay as long as they liked. They were delighted. But for the first couple of nights they stayed at Roz's place in Barra, a beachside neighborhood in Salvador. When they went to Itapoã, we visited them frequently because they didn't know anyone and it was some distance from the city. We were all taking pictures. Jagger was still very young, not yet a worldwide celebrity. He spent most of his time reading and playing drums with the local kids.

Thirty years later, a friend of mine who worked for World Press News Service came to my studio in Manhattan, looking to purchase some pictures. As she was flipping through my prints, she came across an image of Mick in Brazil.

"Do you have any more pictures of this guy?"

"Yeah, about thirteen rolls."

She asked if I would print them. I was too busy to bother at the time. So she took the negatives and had them digitized at her office. When she showed them to her boss, the founder of World Press and a photographer himself, he called right away. I went over to their office and signed a non-exclusive contract to sell the pictures. They ended up being published in France, England, Germany, Russia, Brazil and the United States.

While we were in Brazil, Roz and I somehow got the job of collecting artifacts for a new museum. We met a lot of different artists, including Emanoel Araújo, with whom I became friendly. He showed me how to etch, drawing images with a sharp metal pencil-like object called an awl onto a brass plate. I was able to work in his studio. Today he is considered one of Brazil's major artists. Roz's apartment soon became a hangout for an emerging generation of Bahian musicians, also destined for international exposure, like Gilberto Gil and Caetano Veloso. We were probably the first successful black artists from the U.S. to spend extensive time in Salvador, which is known in Brazil as A Roma Negra, Black Rome. Gil and Caetano loved Miles, Monk, Coltrane, James Brown, Art Blakey and all kinds of black popular music as much as we dug Baden Powell, Tom Jobim, Dorival Caymmi, Gal Costa and João Gilberto. I let the music and culture of this New World capital that had once been a hub of the slave trade flow over me like a cool shower in the tropical heat. My creative juices were stimulated every time I hit the streets. I started writing poetry, making sketches of paintings I wanted to do. I became the Pied Piper of Barra because, mornings, I would walk around beating a little hand drum and scatting sax solos. When I looked around, there were always kids following me, beating on cans and bottles, anything that would make noise. We would end up on the beach, pegando jacaré (bodysurfing) in the warm South Atlantic. The locals loved it,

"Olhem! Aqui vem aquele americano bacana com a rapaziada atrás dele."

(Look! Here comes that cool American with a bunch of kids behind him.)

When Roz's presence began to be known, we were invited to a party at Jorge Amado's house. I didn't know at the time how famous he was. It was a great party. We were welcomed as artists. We toasted each other with caipirinhas, Brazilian rum cocktails. Despite the warm welcome, we soon became conscious that Brazil was not free. The military dictators were admirals and generals who took turns running the country, dissolved the Senate, censored the press, jailed and tortured their opponents and suspended habeas corpus. That meant you could be jailed for smoking a joint. One day, Roz got a phone call from one of our local contacts, letting her know she was on a list of people suspected of doing just that. When the agent came to the door, she showed him around, exuding hospitality. She invited him into the living room, served him a cool drink and, sitting on the steamer trunk that contained our stash, assured him that there was no truth in whatever boatos (rumors) he had heard.

I met a beautiful Brazilian woman, the daughter of a famous painter who became my friend and confidante and took me around the city, explaining the rich Portuguese and African culture that makes São Salvador da Bahia de Todos os Santos inspiring to people from around the world. She took me to a candomblê terreiro on the outskirts of town where there was drumming, the amazingly eclectic altar, the incense, the dancing and singing of the filhas de santo (daughters of the saint), black women in white lace dresses who might at any moment be mounted like a horse by an orixá (one of the pantheon of African deities the slaves brought to Brazil). The swirling energy unleashed by the drumming, singing and dancing made me feel vulnerable. I asked Maria to put her arms around me. That grounded me and I was able to observe the rest of the ceremony without anxiety. The magic and mystery of Brazil has been with me ever since.

Within months of my return to New York, my artist friend Jan Rabinowitz contacted me about the possibility of going to Surinam to photograph the Djuka people, part of the so-called "Bush Negro Nation" in the former Dutch colonial possession north of Brazil. When we got together, Jan told me:

"The Djukas have had little contact with the outside world for centuries. Their culture is what it was when they fled to the forest to escape their

masters. I want you to record it before everything changes."

Her cousin, a successful businessman, financed the trip. Jan had spent time in a Djuka village and made essential contacts. We flew together to Surinam's capital, Paramaribo, where we met our guide Tony and Robert, our interpreter. Days later, we took an even smaller plane to the mouth of the Tapanahony River, where Tony and Robert awaited us. It was a two and a half day trip upriver to the falls. When we started out, I was trailing my hand in the water. "Take your hand out of the water, man!" Robert shouted above the noise of the outboard motor. Then one of the men threw a piece of raw meat into the river. It was snapped up by a school of piranhas. Their jaws were like shears. I never put my hand, or any other part of my body, in the Tapanahony again.

We portaged the boats around the falls and put them back in the water. When we were within earshot, the guides fired several warning shots in the air. These were answered by shots from the village that were our signal to enter. The Djukas had been front line warriors in the war for independence. They were fierce guer-rillas and the Dutch respected them. They maintained a well-stocked arsenal and were ready for anything. As we entered the Djuka village, they greeted us with drumming. There was a cere-mony to mark our arrival. The chief, or "Grand Man," sat on a hand-carved wooden stool with his back to us. To his right was the village shaman, covered with mud and wearing all kinds of amulets made of feathers and bones. To his left, the Grand Man's interpreter, facing us. The Grand Man never spoke to us directly. He would speak into the ear of the interpreter and the interpreter would speak to those assembled. Our interpreter translated what he said to us. Our welcome took at least an hour. Then they showed us to our sleeping quarters, lined with hammocks and mosquito nets. The houses were made of cedar to repel termites. The next night there was another ceremony. This time, the entire community attended. In front, there was a row of drummers with hand drums. Behind them, another row of men with drums at least five feet tall that they played standing up. To the side, laying vertical in a wooden yoke, was a drum at least twelve feet long with a curved stick in a side pouch. In front of all the drummers was a group of twenty or more women dancers who had formed a circle. They had white pimba clay smeared on their faces and trunks. As the drumming reached a fever pitch, the women raised their arms and came close together, ululating. Some approached the Grand Man with whom they exchanged strong hugs and body slaps. Then they returned to the circle and continued to dance. All of this was done in rhythm to the drums. A central bonfire was constantly stoked with wood. When anyone was particularly moved, he or she would grab the curved stick and beat the big drum with whatever they were feeling energetically. There was one old woman who appeared to be nearing her end. She approached the huge drum haltingly and stood before it for a moment swaying to the polyrhythms of the rows of drummers around her. Then she reared back like a pitcher winding up with the curved stick in her hand and struck the drum with such force that it echoed throughout the village. It was the strongest attack of the night and the people acknowledged it with mighty cheers and strident ululations. Then, to my amazement, half a dozen men and women jumped into the bonfire and began to dance among the flames. At that moment, lightning struck, the skies opened, water came down in buckets and people ran, helter-skelter, back to their beautifully carved wooden houses. I was so awed by what I had witnessed, it took me a while to react to the storm. The village was completely flooded and people were yelling joyfully as they ran. Two days after entering the Djuka village, I had witnessed an awesome celebration of life at a remote outpost in a nation that had won its independence in bloody conflict with colonial troops from the country of canals, windmills and tulips I had photographed three years earlier.

Surinamese houses are made of wooden planks, their roofs thatched with palm fronds. The women sweep the village grounds every morning. Everything is kept clean and orderly. The men go hunting for iguanas, monkeys, wild pigs. When they fish, they make a dam of leaves in the river and use a root that stuns the fish but is not toxic to those who consume them. They make a plum-like wine of the fruit they gather in the wild. One of their staples is a fibrous root they call quaka that is grated, heated and formed into rounds that dry to a cracker-like consistency. The first week I was there, I would get up and hang out in the village with my camera around my neck. But I didn't take any pictures. Some mornings I would engage someone in a conversation. At first, it was sign language and grunts. Then I started to say some things in English like "Good morning!" The next time I would see them, they would try to say, "Good morning!" to me. If I repeated the greeting, they would run around laughing, saying it again and again. We were experiencing the joy of mutual discovery. The second week I began to take pictures, first turning my camera to something in which I pretended to be interested before turning it slowly to frame my intended target. As soon as this ruse was unnecessary, I aimed the lens directly at what I wanted to shoot. The Djuka soon grew accustomed to my presence. One day, I sat on a rock and watched the women wash clothes. They smiled and waved. I shot nothing. When they stopped paying attention,

I started shooting at will. All this took about a week or so. Then, they started posing, especially the kids. The point is, they relaxed. I had become part of the landscape. But I was always discrete. The Dutch had tried to build schools near the villages but the people weren't interested, they burned them down. Finally, the colonizers got smart: they dressed Grand Man Gazon in Western clothes and took him to the United Nations in New York. It was the first time he had seen anything like it. When he got back, he gave them permission to build a school by the river. The kids took a boat to and from their village. A couple of times, I went with them, taking pictures in the boat and at school.

There were other tribes in the region, the Saramaka and the Boni. Word of my presence had spread. Someone told me that one of the Boni elders wanted to meet me. Perhaps he thought I didn't exist and an invitation would reveal the truth. One of the Bonis arrived to escort me to their village. I took Robert with me to interpret. It was a couple of hours upriver. When we got there, they took me to a cabin where the old man sat. They brought me a stool and I sat in front of him. For a long while, he just looked at me. I saw tears in his eyes. He spoke to Robert, saying he was very happy to see a long lost brother come home. I let what he'd expressed sink in. Our connection was palpable. Then he asked where I had come from and what was it like there. I happened to have a copy of LIFE with a story entitled "New York and Paris: Fashion Capitals." I handed it to him, he spent a while looking at the pictures, then looked at me with a quizzical expression and started to laugh uproariously.

"Why is he laughing?" I asked Robert.

"He finds it odd that people there live in boxes, one on top of the other."

I realized what modern cities must look like to a man with

a house in a rain forest clearing. I began to laugh, too. Then he asked, "Where are your children?" I told him my children were where I had come from, the United States. It was getting to be early evening, time to go. When he took my hand in his, I was filled with emotion. I felt a deep connection to this man whom I would never see again. Then it started to pour. They hung a hammock with mosquito netting for me in a hut full of people. It was hard for me to go to sleep. I woke up in the middle of the night and realized that I hadn't wrapped the gauze net all the way around me and those sons of guns ate me alive! I looked like a pin cushion with dozens of itchy welts on my back and legs. I think that's when I got malaria because, by the time I got back to the Djuka village, I had a terrible fever. Malaria is a disease I would not wish on my worst enemy. You feel as if you're freezing while your temperature is soaring. You're dripping with sweat and shaking with cold all at once. You can't eat anything because everything comes out both ends at once. I had to crawl because I hadn't the strength to walk. I was in and out of consciousness for what seemed like days. Jan must have gone to the other island to call someone and they sent a seaplane. The next morning I awoke to the vision of a cherubic little white woman, a British nurse, who injected me, saying,

"I have something here that will make you feel better in a trice, ducky! You'll be okay."

It took me a while to focus. Everything was blurry. I had lost myself in a fever dream.

"Are you an angel?" I asked my rescuer.

CHAPTER FIVE

THE BIZ

When I was in high school we would go to parties that were chaperoned by adults. We'd play games like pin the tail on the donkey, musical chairs, and hot potato. I liked spin the bottle, at least in theory. I'd played a couple of times but the bottle never pointed my way. Finally, at someone's party, the bottle pointed at me. I had to go into a closet and close the door. They spun the bottle again and it pointed at Myrna. She was a high yellow gal with a pretty face and a juicy body. When she opened the door, I saw who it was. She closed the door, grabbed me and started kissing me. I didn't know what to do when she put her tongue in my mouth. She was stacked and let me touch her breasts. The other kids were banging on the door:

"Alright, come out of the closet now! That's long enough!"

Flash to Ohio University, fall term, 1956, my junior year drawing class. Our teacher, Mr. Roberts told us that a new model would be posing. We had had a dried-up older white lady the year before and everybody complained. When I entered, I saw a young black woman sitting on the edge of the stage in a royal blue robe. Mr. Roberts said, "Okay, Jackie, we're ready to begin." The young lady ascended two steps to the platform, untied the belt, let her robe fall to the floor and assumed a standing posture with her hands slightly above her head. After a while, Mr. Roberts looked in my direction.

"Mr. Cowans, are you going to draw today?"

There was no mark on my paper. I was transfixed. The charcoal was in my hand but I was immobile. I asked to be excused, left class and went to my dorm room. Jackie was the most beautiful woman I had ever seen. She was chocolate brown and her body was unblemished and perfectly smooth. All of her attractions were round, firm and well-proportioned. I told my roommate I had seen a goddess.

"Really?"

"Really."

Next day as I was walking across campus, I saw Jackie coming toward me and got really nervous. But as she got closer, my panic subsided. I asked her if she would join me for pizza and beer after class. She smiled a big, beautiful smile,

"Sure. What time?"

"Seven o'clock."

I was shaking with excitement.

"She's going to go out with me!"

My roommate couldn't believe it. I picked her up at Voigt Hall, the girl's dorm. We ate pizza but, already drunk on Jackie's beauty, I only finished half a beer.

"I have a car. Would you like to go for a little ride?"

"Sure."

We got in my car and I drove away from campus, into the surrounding countryside. I parked near David Hostetler's house, cut the lights off. We looked at each other and we kissed. The town where my mother was born and where my uncle still lived, Belpre, Ohio, was about 25 miles from campus. I asked Jackie if she would like to spend a weekend at a motel in Belpre. She said, "Sure." That week every time our paths crossed, I would get excited because I knew the weekend was coming. On Saturday afternoon, we drove to Belpre. I borrowed my roommate's Ford because it was newer than my car. I checked into the motel as a single. Then I got Jackie from the car and we entered the room together. This happened more than sixty years ago but it could have been yesterday.

Jackie broke me in, she taught me how to please a woman. She was only at O.U. for one semester. A couple of years later, I came across a picture of her in a photography magazine. I was at Oceana Naval Air Station in Virginia Beach at the time. I stared at it for quite a while, grateful that such a gorgeous, passionate black woman taught me how to make love. In my senior year, I became a big man on campus. Word got around that I was a "good date," someone who listened to and respected young women for who they were, not just how they looked.

My next film I financed myself. I rented equipment from another company. The film was called "Southern Notes." It was about my friend Naima's grandmother who lived in Atlanta. She was a philosopher, a wise woman worth listening to. I thought she would be a great subject for a documentary film. I got the crew together, hired a cameraman, my brother Vincent was handling the lights and equipment, Naima was the co-producer and script girl. We went to Penn Station and loaded everything on a train to Atlanta. A half an hour before departure, the cameraman's girlfriend calls to inform me that he can't go. I say, "Put him on the goddamn phone! Audley, if you don't get your black ass down here right away, I'm gonna kill you!" As the train is ready to pull out of the station, I see him running down the track. My brother helps him on board. I'm already making a shot list for the first day of shooting. The next morning we arrive in Atlanta, rent a van and load it up with the rented equipment. We stay with Naima's grandma because we can't afford a hotel. We bring all the equipment in the house because I don't want a replay of the Sun Ra experience. The next morning we start shooting. I tell Audley to set the camera up for the first shot. I get a sinking feeling when I notice he is having a hard time putting the camera on the tripod. I help him set it up, make sure the film is loaded, adjust the sound, check Grandma's microphone and we shoot the clapboard: Act 1, Scene 1, Georgia Notes, Director: Adger Cowans. Clack! Action! Everything seems to be going smoothly for the first few scenes. I'm directing Audley: "We're going to start on a close up of her hands and pull back a little and pan up to her face." Audley has locked the camera off so it's impossible to pan. I unlock the camera and Grandma says some beautiful things but all we have on film are her hands. At this point there is a flame coming out the top of my head. I figure we can get by with a voiceover and stay on her hands. After a lot of trial and error, I realize that Audley has no idea what he's doing. So, I take over.

Things went pretty smoothly after that. We shot for two weeks in Atlanta and the surrounding countryside. Then we returned to New York to start editing. I took the film to a lab to be developed because we were shooting color. I cut the film down to about twenty-seven minutes. This was old style editing with a Movieola. The people who saw the first cut liked it. But it still needed a final cut, additional sound and editing. I wanted to use jazz and had discovered that you could record up to thirty seconds of any tune without having to pay royalties. I started to look around for grants to finish the film. There was a company in Washington, D.C. that had a grant for young filmmakers. I sent them the film and a lengthy application. I figured we'd hear something in a matter of weeks. Instead, months went by. I made weekly calls to the grant office. They said that a lot of people had applied and the selection process was ongoing. Six months later, I was still calling and getting nowhere. Finally, I got very aggressive and asked them to send back the film, thinking that I could apply for another grant someplace else. They called several days later saying they were sorry but they couldn't locate the film. I realized that I had sent the original and hadn't made a copy. It took the wind out my sails. It was a while before I could put it into perspective. I went back to shooting stills, my own personal work. I was through with movies, movie people, that whole ball of wax. Then I got a call from Sonny Jim, a black actor and playwright. He wanted to film a play he had written. It was called "Hard Head" from the axiom, "A Hard Head Makes a Soft Behind." He said there would be no problem making the film because they already had the money. We rented 35 millimeter equipment, lights, tripods, Sennhauser sound, everything professional. I was the cinematographer and Sonny Jim was the director. We got the permits and started to shoot in Harlem. They even rented a car for my use. We rented a church basement to store all of our equipment and as a place to eat our meals. Our main actor, Bobby, a cool, good-looking dude, was one of the backers. The first day, we shot in Mt. Morris Park. From the first day on set, I realized that Sonny Jim was not a director. The production manager, Harvey, agreed with me and suggested that I accept the dual role of cinematographer and director. I decided that Sonny Jim had to be kept in the loop so I suggested that we co-direct. I would direct and Sonny Jim would help when I needed him. He had really good rapport with the actors because he had worked with a lot of them on other projects and they respected him. Midway through the shoot, things were going fairly smoothly when I got a call from Sonny early one morning saying that Bobby was in jail. You can imagine my chagrin. Bobby was both a principal actor and a major backer of the project. When I asked Sonny what happened, he said

"It's a long story. Bobby took the rap for his boss."

"What are we going to do about the movie?"

"Can we shoot around him?"

"No, we have to shoot all his scenes over with another actor."

"Mr. Cowans, I don't know if we can do that because the money is drying up."

Two years go by. Out of the blue, Bobby calls:

"Where's the footage?

"It's in the Lab and we owe them money."

"I'll pay the bill but I want to have a screening."

We screened all the footage at the Lab. It took two and a half hours. Some of it looked pretty good and some made no sense at all. Bobby paid the bill and took the footage.

Here's what I learned from these abortive experiences: a) have a good screenplay; b) work with people who are proven professionals; c) hire a good producer and, from the get go, have enough money to complete the project. A couple of negative experiences as an independent filmmaker have not dampened my desire to continue to make visual stories.

I had just returned from Brazil when I met Vicki Margulies. She was a dancer by training and was working in the producer's office of "Cotton Comes to Harlem," my first film as a set still photographer. We had a meeting of all the department heads. She asked me what I did and I told I her. We left together after the meeting. I had some shopping to do and she came with me. I bought three silk shirts for which she thought I paid a fortune. I was involved with someone else. When I saw she was interested, I told her I had just returned from Brazil and was no longer interested in American women.

I thought that would dissuade her. It didn't. She always made a point of greeting me when she saw me on the set. She invited me to her cousins' house for dinner. There were a lot of people there. The center of attention was a big table with lox, bagels, chicken soup with matzo balls, cabbage salad, borscht, sour cream, kasha. Her people were so friendly and open, I felt right at home. I had a studio on Lispenard Street, on the border of Soho and Tribeca. Vicki came over to see my work. She had on a little pink dress, and matching shoes. She was petite and shapely, like a dancer. She was about to go to the Venice Biennale. She had worked for Sol Hurok for years. He was about to retire and wanted her to take over his artist's management business. But she was afraid she couldn't handle it. For a number of years, we would get together from time to time.

One day Vicki called me: "Adger, I've known you for years, we've always gotten along well and I'd like to have a child with you. I know you don't have much money. I'll assume financial responsibility but I want you to be emotionally involved with our child." I said okay. I felt good about it. She knew I was a free spirit and had made no demands I couldn't handle. Our daughter was born a year later. We named her Sunya. When she was six years old and Vicki was crossing 79th Street and Broadway, a car came out of nowhere, hit Sunya and smashed into a wall. Vicki gave her mouth-to-mouth resuscitation. The police arrived and rushed them to a nearby hospital. They told Vicki her maternal instinct had saved Sunya's life. She was in a coma for three days and we thought we were going to lose her. When she opened her eyes, she was conscious but not talking or moving much. We asked that she be transferred to Children's Hospital in New Jersey. Her brain stem was damaged. She had to learn to walk, to talk and to eat again. Most of the doctors and psychologists who saw her said she would never again be "normal." Vicki and I visited her every day. She would say hi and talk to us but she seemed not to know we were her parents. After about six months, we were in the hospital recreation room sitting with Sunya, picking out notes on a piano. She looked up at me. "Are you my Daddy?"

"Yes, and this is Vicki, your Mama."

Today, Sunya is a vivacious young woman who will probably be an artist. She loves music, drawing, painting and writing. She's a chip off both our blocks.

I had never considered working on movies. Out of the blue someone called me and said that Sidney Poitier was looking for a photographer to work on a film he wanted to make and that I should go see him with my portfolio. He looked through my book until he came to a beautiful picture of Diahann Carroll, closed it and walked out of the room. Joel, his producer, told me he had a friend at United Artists whom he called immediately and who said he would see me right away. When I got there, the production manager looked at my photographs and said, "This is just the kind of work we need." He was talking about my street stuff. "You got the job." I didn't know what the job was, as I had never worked on a movie before. All I knew was that the pay was good and it was a new adventure. That first movie I worked on was "Cotton Comes To Harlem," directed by Ozzie Davis and produced by Samuel Goldwyn, Jr. As a set still photographer, I realized that you couldn't shoot during the "takes" because the sound department would complain that they were picking up the click of the shutter. So I did some research. I read an article about nature photographers and discovered that they used a special box, called "the Jacobson Blimp," when they shot close-ups of animals in the wild. The blimp was expensive. So I made a deal with the producer, Sam Goldwyn, Jr., that I would pay half and he would pay half but, if I got really good pictures, he would pay for the whole thing. When he saw the results, he picked up the tab. After that, word got around and the blimp became a standard in the business.

Working on film sets was very different than what I was doing before. You had to go to work every day and collaborate with people in different departments. That part I really enjoyed. But I had gotten used to the life of a freelancer with a rep who got me different jobs. Sometimes, I'd do three different jobs in a week. You shot the job, had it developed, made the contact sheets, sent them to the client, they marked what they wanted, had them blown up and, if everything was copacetic, they sent you a check, over and out.

Movie photography was like having a day job: you had to be there every day for a certain number of hours in return for a weekly paycheck. There were two guys in the sound department who told me there was a union I should join. At first, I wasn't interested. When I went down to the union hall to fill out an application, they didn't seem very receptive. That made me press on. Members of the International Photographers of the Motion Picture Industry (IPMPI), Local 644 voted on prospective new members. The first round of the vote to admit me ended in a draw. Then Joe Coffee, a cameraman, called to tell me he had broken the tie in my favor. He felt I should be a member based on the quality of my work, not my color. Being an IPMPI member meant I could work in the movie industry with no restrictions.

One of the first movies I worked on after "Cotton Comes to Harlem" was "Puzzle of a Downfall Child" starring Faye Dunaway and Roy Scheider, directed by Jerry Schatzberg. I had begun to get the hang of things; I enjoyed the work, meeting new people and the camaraderie of a family of professionals who were good at what they did. However, it was difficult to be a black man working in a business that was predominately male and white. Sometimes they would say weird shit to me. I let most of it roll off my back. I was there to do a job and I was being paid. I remembered Mama saying, "Sticks and stones may break my bones, but names will never hurt me." I made a lot of friends and I worked on a lot of pictures. Some of my favorites were "Panic in Needle Park" (1971), "Claudine" (1974), "Eyes of Laura Mars" (1979), "On Golden Pond" (1981), "The Cotton Club" (1984), "Gung Ho" (1986), "Dirty Dancing" (1987), "Boomerang" (1992), "Juice" (1992), and "Night Falls on Manhattan" (1996). One fun thing about working on movies was that I had a chance to be in several movies as an actor. In "I'm Not Rappaport" with Ozzie Davis and Walter Matthau, I played saxophone because the actor who was cast as the saxophonist showed up late. Herb Gardner, the director, said, "Adger, can you play that thing?" I said,

"Yeah" and played a few notes.

"Get Adger into wardrobe right away. He's in the scene."

One morning I was sick when I was working on a movie and I didn't want to go in. So, between takes, I was sitting in one of the extra cars on the set and the next thing I knew they were bringing the cameras over to shoot a scene in that car. They were calling for the actor who was supposed to be in that scene and he didn't show. So the director said, "Adger, you have the perfect outfit on, bring the script, read these lines."

"125th Street, you got a honkey on your tail."

"Perfect. Bring the camera in close. This is a closeup! Roll 'em!"

By this time I was sick as a dog and sweating profusely.

"Makeup! Wipe him down! Silence! Action!"

Everyone on the crew was teasing me between takes.

After the last take, I took a cab home and went straight to bed. I had the flu. The picture was "Live and Let Die" with Roger Moore as James Bond. I survived the cut. If you look for me, you'll find me.

I worked with many directors. My favorites were ones from whom I learned something, just by watching the way they worked. Sidney Lumet, Francis Ford Coppola, John Cassavetes, Bill Duke and Alan Pakula are on that list. I liked them because they were actor's directors. They knew what they wanted and how to get it with the least amount of fuss. Actors I enjoyed working with were Henry Fonda, Anthony Quinn, Katherine Hepburn, Faye Dunaway, Avery Brooks, Jane Fonda, Samuel L. Jackson, Michelle Pfeiffer, Dennis Hayesbert, Wesley Snipes, Calvin Lockhardt, Alan Alda, Ozzie Davis, Walter Matthau, Bob Hoskins, Larry Fishburne, Anne Deveare Smith, Hallie Berry, Tommy Lee Jones, Gloria Foster, Danny Glover, James Garner, Diahann Carroll, Morgan Freeman and James Earl Jones. They were great actors and great human beings. They carried their understanding of the human dynamic both on and off the screen.

Henry Fonda and Katherine Hepburn were old school movie stars who treated the crew with respect. One day, on location for the movie "On Golden Pond," I failed to get a shot because I fell in the water. Henry asked that the camera be moved back to its original position so I could reshoot the scene. The director was livid. Working on movies as a still photographer, you get involved in ego battles. Toward the end of the picture, we had a long weekend break and Jane went back to California. When she returned to the set on Monday morning, she introduced Katherine Hepburn to a young black man who was her guest on the set.

"Katherine, I want you to meet Michael."

"So happy to meet you. Are you famous?"

Half the crew said, "That's Michael Jackson!"

"Oh, it seems you are!"

From then on, whenever time would lag, somebody would imitate Ms. Hepburn,

"Are you famous?

It never failed to break us up.

Jane did a scene diving in the water. Between takes, she sat on the diving board, looking very sexy. I took a picture of her. Later, most of the guys on the crew asked for a copy. When the pictures came back from the lab, I handed them around. Jane happened to see one and confronted me,

"Adger, is that one of your pictures?"

"No, of course not!"

I'm sure she knew it was and liked the fact that her coworkers found her so appealing.

I did another picture with Jane called "Rollover," costarring Kris Kristofferson. We went to Morocco to shoot some exteriors. It was exciting to be back after so many years. I took my son Eden with me so he could experience North Africa. He hadn't been out of the country with me before and he loved it. He was working as my assistant. Some of the extras were people I knew when I lived there. It felt as if I were back where I belonged, in my home away from home. Unfortunately, we ate some food from the Medina and got dysentery. Bernadine, Jane's makeup artist, was with us and she got sick too. Eden and I had a room together, Bernadine joined us and we were miserable together. Finally we found a local doctor who gave us some shots and, in a couple of days, we were back at work. Working on a film crew is a gypsy life style. You get close to people for a few months and then it's over. You might never see them again. I took my daughter Sahru on the set of "The Ice Storm," directed by Ang Lee and, when I introduced her to him, she said, "I know all your movies!" and rattled them off like a true fan. Ang Lee was flattered and asked one of the crew to put another director's chair right beside his. It was fun seeing her sitting there and talking to Ang. I was so proud of her. She's a quick learner and always did well in school.

Working on movie sets is working with a hodge-podge of human emotions, high velocity energy and ego-tripping. In other words, it's a mine-field. Before I started working as a still photographer, Josh Weiner, one of the masters of the craft, took me under his wing and showed me around the set of a film he was working on, "The Angel Levine," starring Harry Belafonte and Zero Mostel. At one point, the two stars started to scream at each other, arguing about something. I thought they would come to blows. The director called a fifteen-minute break and took them into a room. When they returned, all three men had their arms over each other's shoulders, like long lost buddies. Everyone on the set, except me, took it for granted. They were just blowing off steam.

In my years of working on sets, I saw many such incidents. In the end, things were settled quickly and we went on with the next shot. Movie people come from all walks of life. They collaborate with a single goal: to make and market a film that will appeal to as many people as possible. Technology has made global distribution part of the equation. The business requires imagination and strategy, set-building and bookkeeping, a handful of talented actors and hundreds of support people, all of whom must hit their marks every day. Everything has to be camera-ready. The wardrobe department and the makeup and hair people are concerned about how the actors look in front of the camera. After each take, the makeup artist enters the scene and touches them up. The camera department worries about actors hitting their marks and staying in focus. The director is watching their performance. The script department is intently listening to dialogue and worrying about continuity. Those with the responsibility of keeping up with the actors and their movements in the camera department

are the focus puller, the camera operator, and the dolly operator—they have to work as one. For example, if there's a fight
scene and the set is destroyed, all the component pieces have to
be reset before the next take. The coordination of movement on
a set where you have two or more cameras has to be as precise as
ballet choreography. My job, as a set photographer, is to capture
the emotion of a scene in stills for advertising and promotional
purposes as well as providing all the photographs used in the
film. I also take Polaroids of the actors for the hair, wardrobe and
makeup departments and anyone else who requires continuity.

CHAPTER SIX

WAY OUT WEST

I also love the jazz world. I started out as a musician and music is a part of my soul. As Ted Joans said, "Jazz is my religion." I am partial to saxophone players: Bird, Prez, Hawk, Chu Berry, Sonny Rollins and Coltrane, Dexter without a doubt and that big, honkin' man from out West, Gene 'Jug' Ammons, Johnny Griffin, Johnny Hodges, and Sunny Stitt who never quit.

My paintings and photographs are based on musical ideas about rhythm and color. Wassily Kandinsky's theory about the correspondence of music and color becomes evident when you play or listen to jazz. John Coltrane, in the last years of his life, drew mathematical structures that corresponded with sounds. As Sonny Rollins said of Coltrane's rediscovered recording, released in June, 2018 as Both Directions at Once, "It's like finding a lost room in the Great Pyramid." I rarely think of myself as being an artist or that what I do can be called "making art." I am usually focused on translating the spirit entering my subconscious; it's not planned, it's something that happens in the moment and constantly changes, like everything else. We only think, discuss and write about the past or speculate about the future in the ever-changing present. I know I grow quickly bored when I see the same thing over and over. When a jazz musician plays his concept of a tune, it has a living presence or essence that cannot be duplicated. After it's done, you can think about it and attempt to recreate it. That's what the majority of what is commonly considered "art" accomplishes. It recreates the past.

When I listen to music, it isn't that I create from the music. It's difficult to find words with which to describe the artistic process. Art is emotional, not visual. What is the color or shape of the wind? You only know the wind is real when you see how it moves the leaves and shapes the waves of the ocean. We're always using something to say something else. All art is abstract in this sense: after the moment of creation, the emotion that impelled it is fixed. When someone reacts to an image or a film, that's another story. If there's something there and if it's strong enough, it will have a presence and that presence will radiate down through the ages.

People are always trying to understand the artist. You can't understand the artist through the work he or she creates. That's not the point. Save your energy for trying to understand what it is that they present. If I come back in another lifetime, I still want to be an artist. There's no other life for me. I want to be a translator of the spirit, a doorway, a conduit for the ineffable. If you do what you're supposed to do in your lifetime, you don't have time to worry about politics or what other people think of you. The world would be a better place if everyone concentrated on his or her own destiny. As human beings, we are not in charge of the earth. We are here to do its bidding.

The first time I went to California, Tony Batten, a brother with a jazz radio show in San Francisco, told me to look him up when I got there. When I got to the Bay area, I called Tony and asked if I could stay at his place. He said yes. He was interested in photography so I showed him some of the basics. I was still playing trumpet at the time and started woodshedding mornings in his sunny backyard. One morning, a little kid stuck his nose through the fence next door and said, "My mother wants to meet you."

"Where is she?"

"Over there in the window. Look."

There she was, smiling and waving. His mission accomplished, eight-year-old Noah went on his merry way. His Mom, Jodi, told me she had a daughter too and soon Julie appeared, rubbing her eyes and sucking her thumb. We made ourselves comfortable at the kitchen table while Jodi made knots in a cloth she was preparing to dye. I liked her immediately. She was at home in her body and not at all coy. There was a lot of chemistry between us from the get-go. She wanted to know all about me. She suggested we take the kids to the movies. Noah and I were already pals. He was curious about my trumpet, asked me where I was from and if I liked frogs. Next morning as I was playing my horn, Jodi invited me to lunch. We went to the Fillmore that night with her friends, Karla and Carlos. Carlos, despite his name, was a big Irish dude with devilish blue eyes. We got along right away. Karla and Jodi were both artists and got along like sisters. We "decorated our heads" before we went to the Fillmore and took some contraband with us. When we got back to her place after the concert, Jodi said,

"You don't have to go back to Tony's tonight. You can stay here."

Next day, as I was packing my bags, Tony asked if I was going back to New York.

I told him I was just moving next door. Jodi, Carlos, Karla and I were soon thick as thieves. We went everywhere together. I bought a second-hand delivery truck at a Post Office auction for a hundred bucks. We painted it brown on the outside and silver on the inside and christened it "The Brown Rose of Tibet." We made it comfortable for the road with a mattress, a big water jug, tools and camping equipment. I made a bed with a hole for the steering wheel so Jodi's kids could sleep in the front of the truck and Jodi sewed and strung fabric around the front and side windows so we could have our space in back. I put the mattress on a board with hinges so it could be secured like a Murphy bed inside the truck. We began to gypsy up and down the west coast from Humboldt County, Oregon to the southernmost tip of Baja California.

The Bajeños were curious when they came across our little mobile home on the beaches and bluffs of their beautiful state. Jodi's Spanish was pretty good. The sudden appearance of a square brown truck bearing a tall, brown, bearded man in a straw hat, a shapely, smiling Jewish woman in velvet pants and a tie-dye top with two lively kids was irresistible. They would show us where to gather clams, mussels, abalones, oysters. We would awake to find a couple of beautiful red snappers fresh from the Sea of Cortez in the shade of the parachute tarp I devised. Early in the morning when the sun was coming up, there were little bands of color just above the desert floor. As we traveled, Jodi kept a journal, describing our lifestyle down to the smallest detail. We called ourselves the "Flying Pallidinis." Her travel diary, augmented by practical road trip tips, was published as a book, Roll Your Own, in 1974. It's still available on the Internet.

Soon after President Nixon launched the "War on Drugs," we were stopped on the Mexican side of the Arizona border by gun-toting federales who demanded to search the "Brown Rose" from stem to stern. We were traveling with Karla and Carlos at the time and the three smallest kids were in their car with Jodi and Karla. Carlos and I had tucked our marijuana supply under the diaper bags in the back of the truck. All they came up with was a cannabis seed in a plastic bag they pulled out of the air vent. I looked at Carlos, he looked at me and we shrugged. Noah got tense because he had a little Mexican frog in his pocket that he was planning to bring over the border. I hid the wad of cash in my front pocket with my hand. Carlos had hundreds of pesos laid out neatly in his wallet just waiting for the feds to snatch. I went into my spontaneous crazy man routine. When the border guards approached me, Carlos informed them in sign language that I was loco, loco, loco. I took the occasion to jump in the truck and grab a silver flute I just bought, still in its case. I sat on a rocky outcrop, muttering nonsense and clutching the flute. While the federales searched our truck, a group of women and children had gathered. They confiscated three guns Carlos and I bought on an impulse in Cabo San Lucas but they weren't going to lay hands on the flute. I growled like a junkyard dog every time they came close. I'd hug the box to my chest while Carlos reminded them I was loco. When they backed off, I assembled the flute. Still sitting on the rock, I began to play softly and slowly. The kids moved closer, attracted by the melody. The feds split, satisfied with their haul. We got back in the truck. The girls were waiting for us on the other side of the border. When we were rolling again, we replayed the scene, acknowledging our stupidity. We had given the feds their mordida, their piece of the action, in money and guns. Now we were free again to enjoy the landscape and each other. ¡Mejor que la jaula! Better than jail. FANTASTIC!

California had become my second home. I liked the weather and the people and the mellow atmosphere suited me fine. However, I found it easier to make a living in New York. Flora, my agent, was finding me work. I'd work on a movie in New York and then spend time in California, hanging out with Jodi and the kids. Every time I came out west we'd travel somewhere in the truck, camping out. We went to a place called Crystal Lake, near the Oregon border. My water spirit revived, I dove into the clear, cool water with my mouth open—it tasted great. We looked at a piece of land overlooking the Pacific in Humboldt County, Oregon near a river where the salmon spawned. Most of the land in that area had once belonged to indigenous tribes and they considered certain parts sacred because they buried their ancestors there. It was a very peaceful place. The sand on the beaches was black and the waves were a surfer's dream. However, some of the local bigwigs wanted to build an airport in the area. Despite the protests, they went ahead with the plan. The airport opened and within the first few years there were three plane crashes. They decided to close it for good. We camped out on the land for a few weeks, sleeping out under the stars. I had wonderful dreams. I wish now that I had had the resources to buy that land. I still think about it from time to time.

I got a call from New York asking if I were available to work on a film. It wouldn't start for a month. So, instead of flying back east, I got the notion in my head to buy a motorcycle and drive across the U.S.A. It was the year before Peter Fonda's "Easy Rider" was released. We drove back to San Francisco. I went to a leather store and got fitted for a brown motorcycle jacket and brown pants with bone buttons. Then I bought a Yamaha bike. I was too dumb to realize that I should have had a kidney belt made at the leather store. In fact, I thought all I needed was a pair of aviator's goggles and I would be ready to ride. However, one of my more experienced friends insisted that I get a helmet with a plexi-glass shield. That turned out to be good advice because, midway through the trip, I was hit by a stone with sufficient force to crack the shield. I never even thought to check the laws regarding motorcycle safety.

In retrospect, I realize that buying the bike and setting off on a potentially perilous 3,000 mile journey with so little preparation was foolish. But I learned my lesson. In Colorado, I was driving on a twisting mountain road when a guy in a car came dangerously close to my rear wheel. I sped up, hoping I could shake him. However, he sped up too. When I reached a hairpin curve, I jammed on the brakes and slid off the road. The car behind me almost went over the cliff. I was sweating blood. It was that close. There was no way I could have made such a sharp turn at that speed. The asshole behind me made it back on the road just in time and sped away like a dog in a whirlwind. Yet another brush with death. Close to Las Vegas, I thought of stopping. But, as a black man, I knew it might not be the best idea. The night before, at two or three o'clock in the morning, I rented a room in a seedy motel. The place was almost empty. When I got into the room, I had a strong sense that my life would be in danger if I stayed. I climbed out the back window, got on my bike and split. I rode until I found a small wooded area with a stream below the highway and spent the remainder of the night in my sleeping bag. Early the next morning, I stopped at a one-pump gas station in front of a shack. A white man emerged.

"Where y'all goin' boy?"

"Who you callin' boy?," I said to myself.

I was wearing my brown leather jacket, brown leather pants and brown leather gloves. I had bought Frye brown calf-high boots with squared off toes. Jodi had made me a long orange and red tie-dyed silk scarf that I attached to the back of my helmet. It would extend five feet behind me when I picked up speed. Lots of people in passing cars flashed me the peace sign when I passed. But the peckerwood at the gas pump had blood in his eyes, so I kept my mouth shut.

I decided to stop in my home town. I was riding up Broad Street when two cops pulled me over.

"Where you goin', man?"

I told them I was going to my house at 259 Taylor Avenue, adding that I was born and raised in Columbus and that I had graduated from East High School.

"East High? I graduated from there too! What year?"

"Class of '54."

"I was right behind you. Hell of a b-ball team. State Champs."

I wanted to surprise my mother. I knocked on the front door. She pulled back the curtain.

"Who is it?"

"It's me, Adger Wilbur."

"You don't look like no son of mine."

"Mama, open the door!"

"Boy, look at your face!"

I went to the bathroom and looked in the mirror. I was dust-caked and all the dirt had lodged in the creases of my face so I looked like an old man. When I was recognizable, she hugged me, gave me something to eat and I went to bed in my old room. The next morning I rode around the neighborhood in my road warrior outfit without the helmet.

"C'mon mama, I'll give you a ride!"

"I ain't gonna get on that thing!"

But aunt Kate was ready. She got on the back and I rode her around the neighborhood, stopping and starting, taking off fast and tearing up Long Street. She enjoyed every minute, screaming like a teen-ager. The next day, after seeing my family, I set out for New York City and arrived in one piece.

CHAPTER SEVEN

SCRAPPLE IN THE APPLE

I loved my bike. I would get up early in the morning and ride down the West Side Highway to the George Washington Bridge, then ride up and down the Jersey Palisades just for the hell of it! It was my daily ritual and it took about 20 minutes because I stomped on the accelerator and flew like the wind. I was taking pictures for Marvin Silvor, a top-of-the-line window designer. One day I was riding down Forsythe Street, off Houston, and a Cadillac was waiting at the light to turn left. As I approached from the opposite direction, I figured I had the right of way and proceeded straight through the green light. I'll never know if he saw me or not but he turned right in front of me. As I slammed on the brakes, I saw a flash of light and the next thing I remember is lying on my back in the street looking up at the sky. I had wet my pants, I was sweating profusely and my heart beat uncontrollably. I slowly got up, pushed the bike across Forsythe Street to where I was living, parked it, walked upstairs like a zombie and knocked on the door. My friend Elaine opened it.

"What happened? You look strange."

"I thought I was going to die."

I told her the story. She couldn't get over my appearance. There was something she had never noticed about my face, a subtle difference she couldn't describe. What the hell was she talking about? It took me four or five years to recall what had happened: the light went out of me and came back, all in an instant. The voice in my head said, "You're dead!" When the collision didn't occur, the light came back into my body with such force that it suspended all understanding and control. There were a few seconds when I lay on my back in the middle of the street looking up at the sky, not knowing anything. My conscious mind said, "Why are you on your back, looking at the blue sky?" I could see the motorcycle wheel turning on the periphery of my gaze but everything else was cloudless blue sky. My trauma had triggered an out-of-body experience.

When Barbara and I separated, I moved from 331 West 85th Street around the corner to a tiny rooftop penthouse at 340 West 86th Street. We were having marital problems. One day when I came home from work late, Barbara was watching television. She said, "Your dinner's in the oven." She didn't get up. Our son, Eden, had just started crawling. I picked him up and I went to the kitchen and sat down. I removed an overcooked TV dinner from the oven. The aluminum container was burned. Eden climbed up on my lap. I was very depressed and whacked him on his diapered behind for no particular reason. He crawled down the hallway. Sitting alone at the kitchen table, I began to weep. Next thing I knew, Eden was back. He grabbed my leg and looked up at me weeping. He crawled back into the front room and tried to get Barbara's attention:

"Mama, Mama, Daddy Daddy."

Absorbed by the TV, she didn't respond. He crawled back out to the kitchen and looked at me again. I continued to weep. He got back down on his knees, crawled to the living room again and said the same thing, louder. Barbara paid no attention. He crawled back to the kitchen a third time, really upset. He looked at me and back he went to Barbara and started pulling on her dress.

"Mama Mama! Daddy Daddy!"

This time Barbara got the message. She came running out to the kitchen. I was still crying. I was upset with myself for hitting my son because I swore I would never do that after the way my father had whipped us. I was upset with Barbara because she ignored me and burned my dinner. I was upset at how distant we'd become. I didn't want to lose her and Eden, but we couldn't go on this way.

Soon after that, at the penthouse studio on 86th Street, I was sitting on the edge of the roof, contemplating suicide. The pain of what my life had become made me want to die. In my mind, it was a practical decision: I knew there was another world beyond this one and I wanted to go there. Then I heard a voice, calling my name. At first, it seemed far away. I looked around and realized it was Ronnie, my friend, to whom I'd given the keys to my place so he'd have a quiet place to write.

"Ajax! What are you doing, man? Are you crazy? You have so much to give to the world, man!"

"Bullshit."

"Please, man, please!"

The voice in my head interrupted my pity party:

"Adger, who you kidding? You ain't gonna jump. Making drama, that's all!"

Ronnie grabbed my shoulders and pulled me off the roof edge. He had a bottle of wine and we sat in my little penthouse, drinking it and remembering happier times. My 86th Street studio had been a haven. From the rooftop I could see the West Side of Manhattan all the way downtown. If I climbed the ladder to the water tower, I could see the East Side as well. Some mornings, I would sit on the top of the water tower and meditate. I was still living with Barbara and my son, Eden, part-time. One morning, I found the studio door broken open and everything gone: cameras, equipment, lights, everything I owned. I felt exposed and very unsafe. I didn't know what to do or where to go. But I knew I needed to work. I told my agent that all my equipment had been stolen. Then I picked up my portfolio and took the downtown train to Advance Camera run by two brothers, Sam and Lou Fry. It was one of the few places in the city I felt at home. "What's wrong?" Sam asked. I told him and he repeated news of the disaster to his brother. They were immediately sympathetic. They asked to see my portfolio. They looked through it page by page, making comments, all of them positive. They closed the book and looked at me. Then they looked at each other and nodded. Sam spoke first:

"What kind of stuff did they steal?"

"Two Nikons, a 180 millimeter lens, a Tilt All tripod, a nice leather bag, some long lenses, a Weston light meter, a Polaroid camera, a Norman strobe unit, filters, everything!"

"What do you need to get started again?"

Every piece of equipment I mentioned, they placed on the counter in front of me.

"I can't afford any of this. I can't even make a down payment."

"You're a talented photographer. We know you're going to make it. When you make some money you can pay us back. You don't have to do it all at once."

I never bought anything from another camera store as long as Advance was in business. Money was never mentioned again. If I needed anything for work, it didn't matter what, they would see to it that I got it. Whenever I was on location, working on a movie, they sent me anything I needed. They knew I was good for it. I would leave a portfolio at the shop. If anyone wanted to see my work, I would send them over to Advance. I got to know Sam, Lou and their families very well. When my mother would come to town without letting me know and I was traveling, which happened a couple of times, she went straight to Advance because Sam and Lou always knew how to get hold of me. They'd call the set and when I picked up they'd say, "Your mother's on the phone." When the brothers retired and moved to Miami, we'd speak regularly. They always recognized my voice right away. When their sons took over, my credit remained as good as gold. It's hard to explain to people nowadays that such a place and such people existed not so long ago. You'll have to take my word for it.

I was one of the founding members of a group of African American photographers called Kamoinge. Our purpose is to show positive images and excellent photography by and for African American people and the rest of the world and to stem the tide of negative images about people of color that has been diffused by the media for years.

In 1968, I went to Brazil and had a creative breakthrough. When I came back, the European style of painting no longer appealed to me. I painted on the floor, using wood, canvas, metal, whatever. The first technique I came up with was "combing" paints. I would put the colors down and comb through them with instruments I made or found. For instance, I went to the candy store and bought lollipop sticks of different sizes, glued them together and flattened them out and used that to blend the colors together. I also used chopsticks and rubber currycombs they use to brush down horses. I didn't want to use a paintbrush on canvas, I wanted to manipulate the paint itself. I worked on the floor, rather than an easel. I would put layers of paint on the canvas and then comb through them with different instruments. I was also into making paper and casting paint off of glass. I would take a piece of textured glass and cast off of it. These were both techniques I created because I was interested in using paint in a different way. I dreamed up many techniques, some of which I'm still working with today.

I had a similar breakthrough in photography. I had a friend who had a little cabin in New Jersey, on the banks of the Black River, and I went down there for a couple of weeks to meditate and clear my mind. I would sit by the water all day. One morning, sitting there, I saw a snake in the river. He seemed to be sitting on top of the water. We both froze. Then what seemed a ray of light came out of his eye and into mine. I realized he had seen me and felt no more fear. He crawled onto the shore and into the woods. That evening, just before sunset, I climbed up on the roof of the cabin and lay on my back looking at the sun glinting on a large tree. Just then a breeze picked up and the leaves started to shimmer and turn, reflecting the light of the sinking sun. The light on the leaves revealed the face of the Buddha. The next morning when I got down to the water, I began to see images of faces, nature, abstract forms, everything came rushing up at me. I was hypnotized. I don't know how many pictures I took but I was aware that the water spirits and I were communicating. After that, we became one. I could look and feel that the water was connecting with me. For many years I wasn't able to verbalize this feeling of connection. I continue to shoot water today. Sometimes the water photographs look like paintings. The first time I showed them publicly was at Greene Street Gallery in 1981. There were sixteen of them, all 40" x 60." The lack of response to their first exposure at the Professional Photographer's Convention in Coral Cables did not discourage me in the least.

I have been playing for years with reflected light. When I was little and in my grandmother's pantry, the window was a hand-made piece of glass with ripples in it and those ripples reflected the light and made patterns on the wall. I was transfixed. One day, I was sitting in my studio when the light coming through the window reflected off a piece of metal on the floor. I photographed that pattern as it reflected on the wall behind me. I was inspired to devise an instrument with which I could focus those rays and photograph them. I'm continually experimenting, diddling around with things I find and seeing how I can put them to use to make an image. I have come to think of myself as an "imagist" rather than a photographer, a painter or a print-maker because I use all those forms to make images.

In 1972, I moved from my apartment at 340 West 86th Street to a 900-square-foot loft at 136 West Broadway in Tribeca. I was filled with great, fluid ideas of how to use paint on canvas. At that time in New York, artists were beginning to live in large, inexpensive, "raw" spaces. You had to fix them up yourself—install plumbing, sometimes electricity. When you managed to find one at cheap rent you put a pad on the floor or a cot in the corner and left the remainder as raw space you could work in. This was before lofts became a popular thing and people with money drove the price up.

I've always been an abstract artist. African American abstract artists were on the rise in the 1960s and 70s. Painters and sculptors like Mel Edwards, David Hammonds, Al Loving, Peter Bradley, Danny Johnson, Howardena Pindell, Richard Mayhew and others. There seemed to be a rift between the non-figurative, abstract artists and those producing racially specific work, both figurative and non-figurative. But it didn't matter in the larger scheme of things because there were very few African American artists with major galleries and even fewer galleries run by African American dealers. We all knew each other. Sometimes we would get together in one bar or another and discuss our plight.

Neither negative vibes nor rejections from desirable galleries kept us from working at our craft. We had artists to look up to and be inspired by like Jacob Lawrence, Romare Bearden, Norman Lewis, Charles White, Huey Lee Smith, and Elizabeth Catlett. The advent of the digital age and the fact that the Black Arts Movement fought the establishment for so many years has paved the way for younger artists, black and white. When art contains racist elements it deprives everybody of creative possibilities and spiritual advancement.

In my new digs in Tribeca, I was grappling with the idea of paint itself being the vehicle for emotion. The Abstract Expressionists brought forth the idea of emotional expression in paint. Guys like Jackson Pollock, Norman Lewis, Yves Tanguy, Wassily Kandinsky, Arshile Gorky, Kazimir Malevich and many others inspired me. Mornings I would work in the loft. Sometimes, in the afternoon, I would visit other artist friends. We'd hang out in somebody's studio or at a party or an opening. Then I'd go back to my loft and work some more. Sometimes day and night bled into one another. I'd get up, take my camera and just start walking, photographing whatever presented itself to my lens. Manhattan was a living organism with fascinating rhythms. When I was beat, I'd stagger back to the loft and crash. Sometimes my clothes piled up for a month or more. Often, it made more sense to throw the dirty ones away and get new ones. I remember having twenty-five pairs of Levis and fifty t-shirts. I must have had fifty pairs of undershorts and gobs of socks that I threw away constantly because I worked in them and they got covered with paint. There were variations to these patterns when I would go out with someone, get a fashion assignment or a commercial gig or travel out of town. When friends came to the loft they would ask, "How do you find anything here?" because I had piles and piles of things I was working on: collections of artifacts, books on religion, history, art, music, photography, philosophy, psychology, poetry, the science of color, books on sound, autobiographies of great people, books on rare birds and scores of sketchbooks and drawing instruments, plus things that were half finished, sketches of projects I was planning, paints and paint brushes, rolls and rows of canvases, some freshly stretched, others completed, lots of records, musical instruments, a darkroom and God knows what else. I knew where everything was because every pile had its place. In one corner I had built a loft bed and, under it, a darkroom with a small window and an exhaust fan to get rid of the fumes. From my loft bed, I could oversee the madness below. A lot of my friends hesitated to put their stuff down, fearing it would get swallowed by my stuff. But for me it was a peaceful place. I had found it, furnished it and I loved it. A lot of my artist buddies liked it too. Truth is, it was an accurate projection of what was going on in my head at the time.

I was introduced by the painter, James Phillips, to a group of artists whose sole purpose was to make images of and for African American people. They called themselves Afri-Cobra, an acronym for the African Commune of Bad Relevant Artists which started with the "Wall of Respect" in Chicago, where a group of black artists painted pictures of their heroes and heroines. It is primarily a painters' group. The members of both groups were very supportive, like a family. We always critique each other's work in a positive way. Both groups still exist. I was interested in being part of Afri-Cobra because these artists were defining their own destiny. I knew that my painting style was unorthodox and very similar in spirit to the kinds of work the brothers and sisters at Afri-Cobra were doing. I felt that if anybody could understand and critique my work in a positive way it was them.

I think that all artists should read and travel. When you get stuck in a rut, open a book, listen to music, go to a museum or explore something new, it doesn't matter where. It's just the idea of living elsewhere, new sounds, new colors, new foods, new people, new music, all of it can influence you and your work in unexpected ways. Teaching does this too because you usually learn as much from your students as they do from you. It's a win-win situation. What I've learned in all my wanderings is that all humans carry the same blood. We all hurt, live, love, and die. The only difference between the average person and the artist is that the artist is in touch with his or her inner voice. Listen to and express the musings of your inner voice. When you do something good for another person, it flows back to you and you feel good. When you do something hurtful, you feel that too. Concentrate on the positive and eliminate the negative, just like the song says. As for "Mister In Between," he's a drag. As Goethe said, "What is not started today is never finished tomorrow."

I loved to make the rounds of the downtown jazz clubs: the Village Gate, the Village Vanguard, the Five Spot, the Half Note, Bradley's, and Slugs' which was relatively new and where some of the younger players could be seen. Sun Ra and his Infinity Arkestra were featured performers there every Monday night for years. I met Ra at his house on the Lower East Side. The poet Ishmael Reed introduced us. Several other band members were already there: Eba who played trumpet and Marshall Allen who played alto saxophone. When I walked in, Ra was playing a little electronic instrument he had made, the television was playing at top volume as was the record-player. I thought to myself, "This man is tracking three sound sources and a visual all at once. What a creative mind he must have!" Some weeks later, I was walking in Harlem when I came upon Sun Ra and the band playing a gig on the street. I was becoming interested in shooting film so I was carrying a 16mm Bolex. I shot some spontaneous footage of the gig. Later on, I met the whole Arkestra at Sun Ra's house in Philly. I was thinking of making a film about them and heard they were gigging at a band shell in a park in upstate New York. My friend Tommy Mimms agreed that filming them would be a good idea. I rented a professional 16 mm camera and sound equipment and shot a lot of footage of the Arkestra in that park. Tommy recorded the sound. When we got back to New York, I went to see a friend with a loft on Houston Street to ask if we could leave the equipment there because I was afraid to leave it in the car overnight. I ran upstairs, he agreed. I ran downstairs to find the car windows shattered and everything, camera equipment, sound equipment, lights, unprocessed film, gone! I'd been upstairs for less than three minutes. The company that I had rented the equipment from sued me for $27,000. I had no money. All I could do was explain what happened. They were unimpressed with my story. A decade later, they dropped the suit, letting me know they had collected from their insurance company. None of this dampened my desire to make a film about Sun Ra. In July of 1970, he and the Arkestra were invited to St. Paul de Vence, on the French Riviera, to headline an alternative music festival.

We're all supposed to meet at Kennedy Airport. Sun Ra and the musicians with their instruments and equipment arrive two hours early. We're waiting for Tommy Mimms to bring our tickets. He comes back from the counter and tells Sun Ra, "They say we have no reservation." Tommy's beside himself, he goes around collecting quarters for the pay phone. He calls France. It's nighttime so nobody's in. He leaves a message that we're all at the airport, waiting for our tickets. Ra is cool. All he says is "Reach." Tommy goes back to the phone and sits, waiting for a call from France. By this time, we have emptied the soft drink, sandwich and candy machines. We're getting tired. The plane leaves at midnight. Tommy's waiting for the phone to ring. Everyone's sprawled all over the place, sitting or dozing near their instruments. Cochise has a 6-feet-tall drum and he's leaning up against it, his body painted, a little buckskin vest over his bare torso and buckskin pants. The trumpet player has a bright blue head wrap with a shiny blue dashiki, another musician has on a karate jacket with Japanese ideograms on the back, one of the brothers has his hair in corn rows and tucked up under a big Rasta hat. Another brother has a tight brown and white striped suit and shoes, no shirt, no socks, no tee shirt. Another brother has tights with shorts over them and tennis shoes. Their wardrobe choices are far out and colorful, especially their hats and head wraps. Sun Ra wears a long robe decorated with mathematical squares, circles and crosses and a hat in the shape of a square. The dancing girls are arrayed in shiny metallic colors and a panoply of styles. When they announce that the flight is boarding, we get up and head for the gate. Mimms waves us back, "No, no! I reached the guy and he said the tickets would be paid for but they haven't come through yet!" I fall asleep at 1 a.m. on a bench at JFK and, when I awake, the sun is streaming through the windows. By the time the money is wired to Pan Am, it's noon. Our ragtag band of gypsies boards the plane and goes to sleep. When we get to Paris a douanier (customs agent) runs around collecting all our passports.

"Get on the bus! Get on the bus!"

The bus has been waiting for us. It takes us to the train station. Saint Paul de Vence is near Nice, hours away. The festival folks buy baguettes, cheese and cold cuts and hand them out, along with bottles of mineral water. Manna from heaven! Richard, Ra's manager, is still putting our bags on the train when it starts to pull out. One of the band members reaches down and pulls him on board. When we finally reach St. Paul, everybody's hungry again. Cornucopia awaits us. Our hosts are overjoyed to see Sun Ra and the Arkestra, travel-worn but glad to be here on the Riviera! Mimms and I go to Cannes that evening. It's only a few kilometers from St. Paul. We lie on the rocky beach and talk to some people who invite us to party. We visit the Matisse Chapel and spend a wonderful evening drinking champagne and wine, rapping about music and musicians. Then the festival starts. In the multiple transitions from airplane to bus to train, all of the equipment we bring to film the event disappears. The only things remaining are what we carry: an Éclair camera and a single roll of 16 millimeter film. By the time we get to St. Paul, all the juice in the battery runs out. It just so happens that the French photographers are using the same Éclair cameras we have. They have a room where they charge all their batteries. We explain our predicament and ask if we can borrow a battery to shoot the film remaining in our camera since they are charging half a dozen before our eyes. The response is negative. Tommy, with his Chicago gangster mentality, grabs one after the concert starts and the French crew leaves the room. We shoot the concert with their battery in our camera and return it immediately when it runs out of juice. The French guys are upset but what can they do? After a week on the Riviera, we fly back to Paris and from there to New York. I have twenty-five minutes of the Arkestra's performance on film and edit it down to seven. The final shot is Ra playing piano with his back to the keyboard.

CHAPTER EIGHT

OUR MAN IN TANGIER

In 1986, I worked on a movie called "Gung Ho" with director Ron Howard in Buenos Aires, Argentina. The night we got there, we had a party and drank lots of champagne and wine. I hardly slept. When I got ready to go to the set, my eyes wouldn't focus. Close up, everything looked like mush. I thought I'd had too much fun the night before. I went to see the "set doctor." He sent me to a local oculist who conducted a thorough investigation and said, "There's nothing wrong with your eyes. You just need a little help." I freaked out. I didn't ever want to wear glasses, especially because it makes focusing a camera difficult. Nowadays, most cameras have adjustable optimizers. Then, they didn't. My eyesight was failing before I turned 50! I returned to the set with ugly black horn rims on my nose and the camera crew teased me mercilessly. I considered it cosmic payback for all the people I had called "four eyes" over the years. It was also what William Wordsworth called an "intimation of mortality."

I'll be 82 soon. I swear I feel no different now than I did at 40. I love to contemplate a new project. I want to combine all the things I have learned working with people, images, color, emotion, design and intuition by directing a film. Now that I've had a few instructive failures, it's time for success. The power of motion pictures overshadows and incorporates many other forms of image-making. I am inspired by Sam Fuller's book, A Third Face. He was the complete movie-maker, writing and directing his own stories. Like Sam, I'm interested in telling little known stories that touch people's hearts.

You've got to believe in yourself. If you don't take yourself seriously, nobody else will. The energy of belief is incredible. Everyone has it but not everyone knows how to use it. We are all angels, on our way to perfection. As I said before, it's what you believe, not what you think, that enables you to achieve your desire. It's an honor and a blessing to live a long life and to be in good health. Every situation that you encounter in life contains a lesson. We're not here to judge, we're here to learn, to define our destiny.

When my cousin, Lieutenant Earl Sherrard, came home on furlough, I asked him what it was like to be shot down. He was a fighter pilot in WWII and saw a lot of action. He earned the Purple Heart, the Flying Cross and the Medal of Honor. He had been shot down in combat more than once. I asked what it was like. He gave me a blow-by-blow account:

"I got hit. The plane was going down. I swooped over the tree tops. The wings were being torn off the plane by the branches. I was on fire. My arms, legs and face were burning. I thought, 'Mrs. Sherrard, your son is going to die today!' Then the plane hit the water and I blanked out. The next thing I remember was an English nurse pulling me out of the water, and pressing my body into hers to warm me. My whole body was on fire. I could see the burnt flesh on my hands and arms."

Earl was only five years older than me but he had lived a life I could hardly imagine. I never cared for war movies because cousin Earl described what befell him more vividly than any film.

In 1972, I went with Tina to Praia da Luz in Portugal where my friends Roz and Marshall had rented a beautiful house on a rocky cliff overlooking the Atlantic that looked like a piece of sculpture. I gathered my thoughts there, keeping a diary and trying to imagine where I was headed next. Marshall and Roz collected interesting people. A man whom they said was a prince came to visit. He appeared at breakfast wearing a white floor-length silk robe that had been handmade with looped buttons from the neck on down. It blew me away. I had never seen a robe like that. When I asked where it was from he said a word that echoed in my head, stirring up images of glamour, mystery and adventure: Morocco, Morocco, Morocco. In the few days we spent together the prince encouraged me to visit his country. He said it was about an eight-hour drive down the coast from Praia da Luz to Gibraltar where a boat would take us past the famous Rock en route to Tangier. Tina and I drove through the Algarve, Portugal's gold coast. We got visas in Gibraltar and checked into a hotel because the next boat left in the morning. That night I couldn't sleep and took a midnight stroll around the neighborhood. I heard voices and guitars. I found the source—a group of black gypsies who motioned me to join them. Although I spoke neither Spanish nor Arabic, we communicated with gestures and facial expressions. Oh, what a magical night, a precursor to all that awaited us.

When the ferry docked in Tangier, I went to find my friend Randy Weston, the jazz pianist, who had lived there for years. In the Medina, somebody pointed out his house, an old Moroccan castle, which was just up the hill. As I was approaching, I saw Randy's son, Azzedine, carrying two big Moroccan leather bags.

"Where's Randy?"

"Randy? He's already on the boat! We're splitting."

"Right now?"

"Back to the Apple. We've been here a long time."

So much for my reunion with Randy; I knew to let it go immediately and wished Azzedine well. A year or so after I returned from Tangier, Ornette Coleman asked me if I had heard any interesting music while I was there. I told him about the Gnawa people. They play trance music on small horns with reeds, like snake charmers use. Ornette came to Morocco, listened to the Gnawa, and ended up recording with them.

Morocco's magic is timeless and potent. I felt the presence of ancient peoples from the moment I stepped off the ferry. Men riding on horseback, people selling leather bags and herbs. The smell of mint tea and livestock permeated the air. Men were gesturing and crying their wares, "Ají, Ají! Come here. You want hashish?"

They wore multicolored robes, fezzes, and woven skullcaps of every shade and texture. Some of the fezzes, called tarbouches, were red with blue tassels. Robes of an infinite variety of colors and patterns were known as djellabas. The women wore yash-maks, veils, over their noses and mouths so that only their eyes were visible. Eyes, eyes everywhere. My head was swirling with images and an overwhelming sensation of dejá vu. I said to Tina, "I feel like I've been here in another lifetime. Let's get a place and stay." She felt the same way. We got a hotel room and the resident mosquitoes drove me mad. The next morning we met our rug-maker friend at a café. A Moroccan guy passed by our table and motioned me to follow him. As we entered the Casbah, I told him I was looking for a place. He showed me a couple of places with hole-in-the-floor toilets. That wasn't what I was looking for. When I finally found my way out of the maze of the Casbah, the ladies were annoyed that I had been gone so long. I explained that I was on the hunt for real estate and had gotten lost. The rug maker knew a guy that rented houses. The first place he showed us was perfect. It had a big room I made into a studio, a dream come true. It was on the outskirts of Tangier on a hill with a view of the Moroccan countryside. There were no places I could get art supplies so I bought large sheets of blank paper and went to work. I started doing black and white abstract drawings using architectural tools. Later on, I found a place that sold water-based paints and colored them.

Every day was different in Morocco. We would get up early and take my moped to the open market in the Casbah to buy our food. It was an old market. You had to walk through an arched gate, as in all Moroccan towns. One day I noticed a bunch of old skulls on the lintel on top of the gate. I asked Omar, our guide, what that was about. He explained that, when a town was conquered by a warring tribe, they would cut off the heads of the defeated nabobs and display them at the gate. We rode on the buses with the local folks who brought their animals with them: goats, chickens, musicians, mothers nursing their children. We'd give Omar an American dollar and he'd say, "Not that much!" and return with a handful of change. We traveled to Rabat, Meknis, Azouira, Casablanca, and Fez. Fez was fantastic. They called it "the diamond in the desert" because, from a distance, the white buildings glowed in the sun. It was an ancient city with a huge gate and great big vats of the different colors the dyers and tanners used to dye rugs and leather. The dyers' legs and feet were the color of the vats they jumped in and out of all day long. They worked the dyes into the wool and the leather using their hands and feet. Now they have rubber boots to protect them. Back then, life was cheap.

In the Medina, every craftsman had a little shop. You'd walk past a stall where they were making little brass plates, next to a stall where they made babouches, leather slippers, in all sizes and colors, next to a stall where they produced different types of carpets, or headdresses, next to a candle-maker wearing a green djellaba with purple stars on it. You'd turn a corner and run into a table full of animal heads and body parts, goats, sheep, fresh meat with entrails dangling, skinned rabbits ready for roasting, ears, tongues, eyeballs, a vegetarian's nightmare. Everything impressed me and influenced my work. There was a mathematical precision in the patterns of the tiles, the rugs and fabrics, and the more ornate skullcaps that was visually stimulating and made its way into my dreams. One day, I was in the studio working at my 4 x 12' marble-top table, an ocean breeze blowing through the jalousied doors that opened onto the patio. I had taped a National Geographic map of the world to the wall. Hashmi, the houseman, asked me, "Monsieur, where Morocco?" I pointed out Morocco on the map. He gazed in wonderment. I put my finger on Tangier. He couldn't make the connection between the word, the map and the place where he was born. The next day, he brought a couple of his keif-smoking buddies to the house and pointed at the spot called Morocco with great pride. Some days Hashmi rode with me to the market on the back of my motorbike. He rode sidesaddle and, once he overcame his initial trepidation about falling, he loved being seen by his friends to whom he waved vigorously. When I tooted my horn, it was even better. When we got to the market, I would drop him off to shop and go to a nearby café to eat yogurt and drink mint tea while watching the nonstop street show. After I had been living in Tangier for a few months, I adopted the native garb. Light cotton inner garments made the wool djellaba bearable. I also wore babouches and a skull cap. When I pulled the hood of my djellaba down and put on my shades, I became Everyman. I would hang out watching the locals hustle the tourists. "Good price for this. Good price for this. Hashish? Keif?" It was just pressed-together herbs that looked like hash. One day, some young street brothers rolled up on me. They had me pinned.

"Hey, man, where you from?"

"I'm from New York City."

"Yeah! James Brown! Stevie Wonder! Little Richard!!"

"Yeah, man!"

"Hey man, c'mon!"

They gestured for me to follow them. They took me to a place off the main drag where there were no tourists. It was their hideout, their clubhouse. They wanted to know everything about me. When I told them I was an artist, they seemed to understand. They identified with my adventurous spirit. We drank beers and smoked keif. We were brothers.

A few months later, I was strolling through the Medina. Out of the blue, people started pointing at me and yelling in Arabic. I didn't understand what they were saying but I felt their rage—I was a menace to society, the devil incarnate! People came closer, shaking their fists in my face. It looked like I was going to have to fight my way out of there. I assumed a judo stance, ready to do battle. Just then my street buddies appeared, pushing and kicking people out of the way. They shielded me from my would-be assailants, who fled. The next thing I knew I was back at the gang's hideout. Close call!

One thing that disturbed me was the way women were treated. I saw a man kick his companion's butt for not keeping up with him. She was carrying a heavy load of wood on her back and all he was carrying was a cane. The first week that Tina and I were in Tangier, we made friends with a Frenchman and his wife. We were walking around the Medina together, digging the scene. The woman was wearing shorts, high heels and a little blouse. She looked very sexy. I noticed the men leering at her as we passed. After we parted company, we heard the Frenchman yelling, "That's my wife, my wife! Put her down!" We turned just in time to see several men running away with the woman rolled up in a rug. All you could see was her feet sticking out the end of the roll. Her husband and I pursued them, shouting for them to stop. When they saw there were two of us, they unrolled the rug and ran. Kidnapping tourists in broad daylight? Moroccan madness.

Tina always looked and dressed like a lady, curly black hair to her shoulders, bracelets from wrist to elbow, and carried a white handkerchief. One evening, a little street kid grabbed the handkerchief and took off. I chased after him and cornered him.

"Give me back the handkerchief, man."

I was looking at him strongly. Moroccans always respond to a direct gaze. The kid gave me the handkerchief and pointed to my face.

"Okay, snake eyes!"

Tina was an admiration repository. She had at least three proposals of marriage. The fact that I was at her side hardly mattered. One day she returned to the house and told me a handsome young tradesman in one of the market stalls was sweet on her and had cut off a lock of her hair, with her permission.

I suggested that he might be planning to use it as some kind of juju, went with her to see him and politely insisted he give the hair back.

We were not allowed to bring Omar, our young Berber guide, into our hotel room when we went to Fez. He had become a friend by then and we were prepared to be indignant on his behalf. But he knew the rules and didn't want us to make a scene. Late that night, we brought him into our room the back way so he could sleep on the couch and take a shower in the morning. We didn't want him to spend the night on the streets of Fez. But he'd always leave early in the morning and climb over the back wall. The front gates of the hotel were locked at night. Omar was our link to reality and our stalwart defender. When Tina, unsupervised, bought something he always asked what she had paid for it. Usually, it was far too much by Moroccan standards and he would insist on bringing it back to the shop where she had purchased it. He would yell at the merchant and ultimately get the price the Moroccans paid, pennies to the tourist dollar. We stayed in Morocco almost nine months and Omar was our companion, host and guide the whole time. He had been a seaman and traveled the world. He spoke good English and would introduce us to people he knew and crack us up with his stories. He accepted no money other than his pay. When Tina cooked, she cooked for the three of us. Before we left, we bought him a beautiful djellaba and I left him a lot of my American duds because he liked the way I dressed. Omar helped us carry our boxes and suitcases to the dock and hung around till we left.

The only meat we ate was chicken that we bought from the chicken man. He liked us because we were young, interesting-looking people and bought two chickens every week. One day, when Tina came back from the market, she said,

"The chicken man looked at me strangely when he handed me the chickens. He didn't come onto me but everything about it was weird."

"I don't think you have anything to worry about. He always treats us like friends."

I went back to what I was doing. Tina was preparing to make dinner. Then I heard her shout "Oh, my God!" and ran to the kitchen.

"Look!"

Inside one of the chickens, was a big black ball of hashish.

What Tina interpreted as his odd expression was just his way of letting us know that there was something extra in our order. I suppose it was his way of thanking us for our business. His stall was closed the next day. Someone whispered that he had been arrested for selling contraband.

During Ramadan, we would fast all day and have our one meal after sundown. Tina had picked up a lot of new recipes, including one for hashish candy that is very popular in Morocco.

Our Moroccan visa was about to elapse after three months so we went to Gibraltar, got our visas renewed and came right back. We had gotten to know some of the people in our neighborhood and they treated us like relatives. We went to a lot of celebrations. Tina was a great mixer. People loved to watch and listen to her. Sometimes I went along, other times I preferred to stay home and work in my studio. When we started to run out of money, our friend the rug maker introduced me to the librarian at the American Embassy. She was instrumental in arranging an exhibition of my paintings. We had a small opening and I sold two pieces—that allowed us to stay longer. Finally, in spring with the jasmine blooming in the moonlight in the yard of our rented house, we bought two $75 passages on a Yukalinea freighter from Tangier to Boston with two suitcases and hauled aboard fifteen cardboard boxes full of miscellaneous stuff. The first night on board was memorable. The sun was setting as the boat pulled out. I went below deck to take a nap and, when I awoke, we were already on the high seas. I looked out a porthole and the horizon was at a right angle. I got very seasick. Tina, unfazed, had dinner at the captain's table while I moaned and barfed below. She brought a plate of food for me and the sight of it made me retch. I was sick for most of the trip. One morning when I thought the worst had passed, I decided to try to eat breakfast. Everything was okay until the boat slammed into a trough of water just as the eggs were served. On the next to the last day, I came up on deck and, for a few hours, was able to enjoy the view. When we docked in Boston harbor, Tina's sister was waiting for us. We loaded up her station wagon with the fifteen boxes, the rugs and suitcases. As we were about to drive away, two crew cut customs agents who had been watching us struggle to fit everything into the car gave a short blast on their siren, pulled out their badges and informed us we had to submit to a search. They went through box after box, opening, examining, sniffing around and asking questions. One box was filled with Moroccan spices. The agents' curiosity was piqued. They asked how long we had been there and what we did to sustain ourselves. When they started the search, Tina opened a large tin of candies and brownies she had made and asked the officers if they wanted a piece of Moroccan candy. Everything was coated with powdered sugar and laced with hashish. "No, thank you." She closed the tin and put it in the car as they continued to search. When they were finally satisfied, we reloaded the car and drove off. Tina shook her head: "I sure wish they had tasted a piece of that candy." She was my kind of gal. We laughed all the way home.

CHAPTER NINE

FULL CIRCLE

When you commit to being an artist, your creative life is ruled by emotion—that invisible energy that runs life. Logic comes to a dead end in the creative life of an artist. You cannot judge yourself by other peoples' standards or ideas. You must follow your own intuitive spirit, trusting and following the part of you that dreams.

Abbey Lincoln, Earlene and I were a threesome. We would go with Abbey to her different gigs in NYC and hang out afterwards. One concert in upstate New York was held at a skating rink-turned-performance center where jazz musicians played. When we got there, people were assembling and there was a buzz when Abbey came through the door. She went backstage. Earlene was wearing a little red pillbox hat with a veil and red feather earrings, a white tuxedo jacket with tails, skintight white pants and red spike heels that made her taller than my six-foot frame. She was a knockout! I held my arm out, she laid her hand on it and I led her around the entire floor like my prize possession. People yelled and screamed:

"Mercy, mercy, mercy!"

"Woo-wee! You lookin' good, mama!"

"Do it! Just do it!"

Abbey sang her heart out that night. It was a young crowd and they responded to her interpretations of jazz standards because they knew she was a committed master. Abbey was also a pretty good painter. I organized a group show and included a couple of her pieces because they were full of spirit. The show was called "Works on Paper."

I first met Abbey when she was performing with her husband, Max Roach, at Lincoln Center. Sometime later I was working on a movie called "Nothing But a Man" directed by Michael Roemer and Bob Young. Clayton Riley and I were working as assistants, synching up dailies. We had both read for a part in the film. They told Clayton he was "too light and had green eyes." They liked the way I read but "my nose was too straight and my forehead was too high." They were looking for someone with darker skin, a wide nose and thick lips. They had scheduled Robert Hooks to play the lead. Clayton and I put our heads together and came up with Ivan Dixon and Abbey Lincoln as candidates for the lovers whose story is the focus of the script. Bob and Michael had never heard of either one but agreed to bring them in for a screen test. Abbey's test was magnificent. They liked that she wore her hair "natural" and they thought Ivan was great. There was lots of chemistry between them. They were cast then and there and the picture was a success. It was an American film, an unapologetic love story with black characters in real-life settings. Abbey played a minister's daughter and Ivan a man who worked on a railroad gang, laying track. Later, Michael credited Clayton and I with "casting" the leads.

I worked with Abbey for more than twenty years, photographing her in concert and at recording sessions. We had an artistic camaraderie and a deep respect for each other's work. I knew how to make her laugh. When you thought you knew who Abbey was, she would surprise you. Sometimes, she was human and compassionate and, at other times, she needed a lot of attention and compassion. If you love someone, you accept who they are, whatever their moods or circumstances, and I loved Abbey.

One afternoon, I got a call from Earlene saying that Abbey had been rushed to the hospital and I should go there right away because she wasn't cooperating with anybody. "She'll listen to you," Earlene said. When I got there, I asked everyone else to leave the room. As soon as they left, Abbey said, "Adger, push the bed against the wall." I did as she asked. "Now help me get out of this thing. I'm going home."

"Where you going, Abbey? Where you going?"

"I'm going home."

She tried to get up. There were intravenous tubes in her arms and legs. I said, "Just get back in the bed. You're too weak to go anywhere." It turned out that the reason I was there was to convince her to sign a release form that would allow the doctors to operate. I sat on the edge of the bed and looked directly in her eyes, "Do you want to die?" She made a face like a defiant child but said nothing. Finally, she relented and signed the papers. She made a full recovery.

My friend Nelson Stevens was teaching art at Amherst and his students produced a monthly magazine called "Drum." One day he picked me up in Manhattan and we headed up to Max Roach's home in Connecticut. He asked me to take some pictures of Max for Drum. When we got there, Max was very gracious but he was dressed in everyday clothes. I asked him if he could choose something special for the shoot. He returned in a custom made tuxedo. I wanted to be outside so I ended up photographing him in a natural setting, dressed to the nines. Around the same time I went with Nelson to Max's pad on Central Park West. Nelson bought a big bottle of cognac for the occasion. Max was having a manicure and a pedicure and told us he'd be finished shortly. When he was done, we gave him the bottle. He took it into the kitchen and yelled out, "You guys want something to drink? I got some beers." Nelson's face went blank for a minute. When Max came back with the cognac and the beers, we sat around laughing and talking. He showed us a beautiful, hand-inscribed scroll on parchment he had recently received as a testament to his "musical contribution to humanity" from the University of Bologna, which has been functioning continuously since its founding 970 years ago.

In 1963, Judy James hired me to photograph the play "In White America," starring Gloria Foster and Moses Gunn. The play went on to win several awards. Judy and I became life-long friends and, fifty-five years after we met, we're working on a film together. It's about the 1921 race riot in Tulsa, Oklahoma. I'm committed to this film because it reopens one of the most egregious chapters in the clandestine history of racism in America. It's based on a book by Fred Williams and we're in the process of raising money. I have faith that this film will be made and released.

I was called to work on a movie that was being directed by Ernest Dickerson who had been Spike Lee's cinematographer. This was going to be his first time directing. The cast of "Juice" included Tupac Shakur, Kahlil Kain, Omar Epps, Queen Latifah and Samuel L. Jackson. We shot the whole thing on location, a lot of it in Harlem. I found "Pac," as we called him, to be a very sensitive young man. His lyrics and poems are filled with emotion and beauty. I was amazed when I read he had been killed. Like a lot of our young black geniuses he was to die young—a brilliant flash and then darkness. I also worked with Rakim, one of the original rappers, on an album cover. Our first conversation was about John Coltrane and how important he was to Rakim, who had based some of his rhythms and music on things he heard in jazz. I worked on another movie with Queen Latifah, "The Cookout." She was funny, loving, gregarious and filled with positive energy. I worked with Dr. Dre and Ed Lover on "Who's the Man?" directed by Jonathan Demme. Although we are generations apart in terms of our influences and vision as African American artists, their music is rooted in the black experience and as germane as anyone's to the ongoing struggle.

Sometimes when you're inspired, you start something. You don't always know how it's going to turn out. You're semi-conscious when you're working. So when you take a break or stop and step back from it, you're surprised, sometimes, at what has come through you. It may not always connect right away but a work of art always reveals its deeper meaning when you have lived with it for a while or experienced it. Like most things in life, they become more beautiful when they're used.

Romare Bearden used to say that an artist is like a whale, swimming with his mouth open gathering all kinds of nutrients and then going off somewhere to digest them. That's the way the artist experiences life, gathering emotions, sounds, colors, setbacks, rejections, dreams and joys, and mixing them all in the blender of his soul. The result is often a mixture of experience and intuition that fuels the imagination. Sometimes, it results in a painting, an image, a dance, a poem, a song, depending on your discipline. One thing is sure: being an artist, you have to stay committed to what you believe. For me, it's all about image. Whether it's painting, photography, or print-making—the important thing is to transfer my spiritual energy into an image. There's all kinds of things you can use. Artists these days are using installations, combinations of painting, photography and sculpture, experimenting with other forms of expression than paint. All forms of image-making are cool. David Hammonds is a master of installations. He did an installation at PS 1 where you walked into a large room he'd made into a black box with a curtain. When everything went black, old time spirituals started to play. When you looked up, the ceiling was covered with glow-in-the-dark plastic Jesuses with a fan blowing them so they seemed to be flying, maybe five hundred or more, moving in time with the music. In the sixties we were both doing "body prints." Hammonds was using his own body doing things like "Ace of Spades"—a life size playing card with his own image raising a revolutionary fist as the Ace. I was just rolling big nudes in acrylic across canvases. Nobody was paying me any particular attention but I was having a ball. Hammonds studied with Charles White in California, as did Kerry James Marshall.

I went to the Charles White retrospective, "Truth and Beauty," at MOMA recently. I had seen his work in books but when you see the actual pieces, life size, it's impressive. He is not only a master of his craft. He's also a master of emotion as it relates to people of color. His work, to me, has a black aesthetic. You understand the power and the range of emotions in his works. Black Panther, the movie, had little signatures in it that only a black person could relate to—the power of black women as warriors, for instance. We know that black women are powerful but this was a visual confirmation of that fact. There's a call and response in Charles White's work that's specific to the black experience in America. John T. Biggers' monumental work is from the same era as Charles White's but he includes African and African-Atlantic motifs. Nelson Stevens, one of the original members of Africobra, is the spiritual and visual heir of both Charles White and John Biggers.

At Ohio University, I was a photography major and never gave a thought to painting. What finally got me into it was the idea of doing something else with my hands and making a painted image on a two-dimensional surface. I tried painting figuratively but it just didn't work. I tried painting abstracts with oils but that was too laborious. I wanted to make an immediate image using paint. I liked all the painters, classical and modern: the French Impressionists, the Italians, the Flemings, the black Americans, Charles White, Jacob Lawrence, Romare Bearden, Van Gogh, Titian, Leonardo, Rafael. There wasn't a painter I didn't like. But the one who moved me to express myself as an individual was Kandinsky. His book, The Spirit in Art, made me think about painting in a different way. It was the desire to do something with paint itself. I wanted paint to be the subject. I didn't want my work just to be decorative. I wanted to make images that would capture the mind and jumpstart the imagination. At first, I wasn't sure about the images I was making. I found that, if I put something up in the studio and its effect on me lasted for more than a week or so—I wanted to figure out what it was that kept drawing me back. That's when painting became totally emotional for me. I figured if it affected me, it might affect others. So I invited people into the studio, not people associated with the Art World but just ordinary folks, to see what they were drawn to. That led me to understand that there was something in the work that attracted people, it appeared to be a kind of energy that was radiating from the canvasses. People would say things like, "I really dig it—but what is it?" My images were not readily identifiable, like an orange on a table or a bird. They were just pieces of paint on canvas. The paint invited people to use their imaginations. The more they looked, the more they connected with what they saw and were reminded of things that they could relate to. Other people said, "This is not painting, man. I don't know what it is but it's not painting." Usually comments like that came from other artists. "This is not painting, you're just smearing colors around!" I'm always interested in what people have to say. I put anything that came to mind on canvas. I opened the wellspring of my mind and blew the doors off my imagination. That's when I started to develop my own visual language.

"What's your process?" People love to ask artists that. My process? If I had a process I couldn't really write about it because when you write about something that has the immediacy of life and the instantaneous combustion of imagination, it dies before it reaches the page. It doesn't matter when a work was created— the moment of cognition is what matters and that should last forever. If people say about me when I'm no longer here to defend my art, "Well, Adger was basically just a paint-smearer" and they're still looking at my smears, I'll be content. Basically, it's all about the transfer of emotion.

My dream as a young man was to live like my father and grandfather; they had big families and took care of them. I thought I was going to be the patriarch of a family of creative people, I could teach some of my skills and techniques to my children and grandchildren and we'd travel around the world being artists. But fate had something else in store for me. When that fantasy began to unravel, I didn't have a backup plan so I followed the course of my life as it presented itself from day to day. Some days were harder than others. Who was I to presume that I could make something that other people would want or could use in their lives? I had problems accepting myself as an artist. Or what people called an artist. I actually saw myself as an oddball in society. Sitting around the studio making images was better than having a job. I didn't want a job, ever. In some ways, I feel lucky to have the life I have. But there was something inside me, driving me, that I couldn't understand. It wasn't until I was into my fifties that I came to accept myself as an independent, creative person.

My father didn't care what other people thought about him. That was evident from the way he dressed. When he came to junior high school to talk to the principal about my not standing up for the Star Spangled Banner and Pledge of Allegiance because, the week before, I had seen pictures in the paper about black men being lynched by the KKK in the South, he had his work clothes on because he'd just come from the farm. I was embarrassed. He nodded as the principal spoke. I was standing at a distance watching their faces. My father seemed to be agreeing with what the principal said. When the conversation finished, father said, "Get in the car." We went home and nothing more about what transpired that day was ever discussed. I figured I was going to get hit upside the head. But my father didn't punish me. The next day, I stood up for the Pledge but my heart wasn't in it. I didn't believe any of it anymore. Seeing the picture in Jet of Emmett Till's mangled body opened my eyes for good. I decided to go to Mexico, marry a beautiful girl like my friend Benito Perez's sister, and fight for freedom.

The American Dream wasn't meant for people like us and my father knew it too. My life as an independent young black man had begun. I started to look at people differently. That's when my Uncle Wilbur became larger than life to me. He was a rogue, a world traveler, a hobo who hopped trains across country. He was always on the road, going somewhere without any visible means of support. But he made it from place to place because he was a creative being. That's what I wanted to be, although it took many years for me to feel I was one.

Having been an image-maker all my life, I want to get involved in making movies. Producing, directing, cinematography—it all interests me. I've already made two short films, Water and Pria's Daddy. Now Judith James, Laurel Stradford, Fred Williams, and

I are collaborating on the Tulsa film.

In 2001, I was invited by Dr. George Preston to submit work for the Florence Biennale of Contemporary Art. I was accepted and I packed together six photographs, 40-inches x 60-inches—two nudes, two street scenes and two still lifes. I had to put them on a cargo plane. I raised money to do this by having a sale of my photographs at my friend's house in Harlem. It was exciting to be in Italy, especially in Firenze, with its museums and architecture—the Duomo! I was accompanied by my friend Mahmoudah. The show was up for a month. Every day I'd go and sit with my work, I had a book for people to sign in, I met people from all over the world. I'd go around the convention center every day to see my fellow artists' work. I met many wonderful artists and received the Lorenzo II Magnifico alla Carriera award in recognition of a Distinguished Career. One day, two older Italian women who looked like sisters stood in front of one of my nudes for quite a while. Then, suddenly, they both raised their arms and mimicked the contours of the figure before them, exclaiming joyously "Que bella!" I was so moved that I hugged them both. Their enthusiastic appreciation meant more to me than the award I received.

I had been in Sicily before, in 1998, as part of a show called "African American Artists" at the University of Palermo. I heard that Francis Ford Coppola was shooting a movie at Fellini's old studio, Cine Città, in Rome. A couple of other artists in the show and I took the train to Rome, got a cab and went to the Studio City. My friends disbelieved me when I said I wanted to see my friend Francis. When we got to the front gate, I gave them my name. They telephoned the sound stage, got his okay and we walked a block or two to the set. When we arrived, the red light was on, which meant they were shooting. As soon as the light went off, we walked right onto the set, Francis saw me, said, "Hey, Adger! What are you doing in Italy?" and gave me a big hug. My friends couldn't believe it. Francis said, " Sit down. I've got to finish this scene." We watched a couple of takes, Francis came back to tell me he was glad to see me but had to go back to work. We said goodbye, walked out of the studio, went to the train station, returned to Palermo. When we got back, they could talk about nothing else. "We met Francis Ford Coppola!" They were wagging their tongues for days.

I had a working relationship with Francis on "The Cotton Club." He liked the photographs I shot on set and had a few of them hanging in his trailer. One of them, of the actor Bob Hoskins, ended up in the permanent collection of The National Gallery in London.

Freedom to release your inner spirit: the face that only you know. The face you don't show to others. That's the face that you have to face in order to be a free, open-hearted human being. There's only one heart and one blood and we all share it. When you're born, the first people that influence you are your parents— everything you know comes from them. When you leave home, you begin to restructure your life based on your own experience. You're influenced by other people. When you see people who have done something that you're interested in and have done it well, you want to know more about them. When you're moved by something, you bring that into your life and if it works for you and makes you feel good, you keep it and radiate it. That's an exchange of energy, powerful energy! If you give a person something good, sweet, loving and beautiful from your heart and it touches them, they give it back. You have to be forgiving. Love lives in forgiveness. Hate lives in anger and confusion. I've seen this play out again and again. I've seen friends of mine die of anger and their faces show it.

I used to dream that when I died it was just going to be light. Once I had a dream about a beautiful woman who put her arms around me and loved me. In the dream I didn't see her face. When I woke up I was no longer lonely, I was in tears. In times when I have been deeply troubled about something, these spirits come and console me. If you don't stand up for yourself in this world, if you don't define your own destiny, someone else will. There's no lack of anything in the universe. Lack is an idea that man came up with. All this human stuff that we think is real, is not. We think we're doing this ourselves but in fact it's the spirit moving within and through us. Life is beautiful, wonderful, sweet and tasty. Feel it, love it, have it. The creator made it for you. We're all angel spirits in the making. Don't let anything come between you and that juicy moment. Don't question beauty when she comes knocking on your door. Open it up and let her in! When I was young, I loved to watch the sun come up. It was like the shadows were thirsting to have it shine on them. For a brief moment at sunrise you cannot help but feel good. That's what creativity is like, the sun rising in your spirit, awakening possibilities.

There's nothing wrong with joy. "They made a joyful noise unto the Lord." When you rejoice you re-juice your spirit. Learn a new song, radiate joy, send your positive energy through the ethers! Concentrating your energy means putting it all in one place. Spirit exists in everything, its living essence is in the universe and the human body is its temple. Actually doing whatever it is you are thinking of doing is very important. A lot of people hear the call but only a few rise to the occasion. Take action, positive action around and about the things in which you believe. Don't abuse Mother Nature by putting plastic in the ocean. I'm making art out of discarded plastic bags and candy wrappers these days. The process is laborious but few things I've done have provided me with so much joy.

Last night I was thinking about my childhood again. I know it was the love and the care I received from my mother and my father that gave me the courage to do what I've done. I always felt I was two people: the outside one everyone sees, the physical me, and another something inside of me, an inner guide. It isn't me. It's the spirit within me. When I mentioned this to my family and friends, they looked at me strangely so I decided to keep it to myself. One thing I'm sure of, age is not a deterrent to the creative process.

ADGER COWANS

For speaking engagements, book signings,
appearances, and interviews, contact...

NADIRA HUSAIN

(646) 228-4580

nadira@manhattanpartnersmedia.com

adgersart@yahoo.com

www.ingramcontent.com/pod-product-compliance
Lightning Source LLC
Chambersburg PA
CBHW020914090426
42736CB00008B/637